A book enters the world with help from many.

I therefore wish to acknowledge and thank Virati Nathini for the cover design and layout and for reading through the proof a number of times and making important suggestions and corrections.

Thank you to Narissa Doumani and John DuPuche for reading a proof and offering suggestions that improved the final book.

Much gratitude to all others who contributed along the way.

Keith Simons

GlobalQuest Publishing
PO Box 89, Warburton VIC 3799
AUSTRALIA
globalquest28@gmail.com
Copyright © Keith Simons 2017

All rights reserved. No part of this publication may be reproduced in any form without the written permission of the publisher, except for brief quotations embedded in critical reviews and articles.

Creator: Simons, Keith C., 1949- author.
Title: Biography of a Russian Yogi / Keith Simons.
Subjects: Spiritual biography, Tantra, Yoga.

ISBN 9780975836521

*Why can we not find the whole
universe within ourselves?*

Only wise people can allow meditation.

Foreword

In actual fact, many touched on the topic of writing my biography, even during the time when crucial events of my life hadn't finished. But it turned out that those who mentioned this were not deep enough to do it, and I simply didn't have time for writing my own biography.

Even now there is a lack of time, but somehow suddenly, with very unpredictable consequences, Keith Simons, my good friend in Australia, offered to write a book about me by way of a dialogue with him. I must say that I immediately found a common language with Keith. He is a very deep and open person with great erudition, communication, talent and gift as a writer. He facilitates group meetings in Warburton, his home town, where people try to become more aware of their multi-dimensional nature through deep listening and meditation. Once he invited me as a guest speaker (he jointly facilitates this as a fortnightly group with different guest speakers each session) to share about my experiences. When I told him about my life, he thought and said, "There is a need to write your biography, for sure". I looked at him and thought, 'This is so, and it is the proper time for it to be done'. Moreover, I am a man of experience, and for me the format of communication that Keith suggested felt to be most convenient. Many thanks to him!

Of course it is not always possible to cover everything within one book, so some events are set out in the form of their essential significance.

This book can become food for reflection. It doesn't contain fantasy or exaggeration but, as it strikes me, an account of an ordinary and real life is better able to 'shape the brain' in a balanced way. The main topics which most people have to deal with in one way or another are touched upon in this book.

I hope reading about my life story will be interesting, inspirational and useful to you.

Enjoy reading!

Yogi M

CONTENTS

Introduction 11

PART 1 RUSSIA

Beginnings 17
Matsyendranath 19
Maxim the Artist 21
Shifting Sands 26
Childhood 29
Bryansk 34
Birth Trauma 37
Black Sheep 38
Collapse of the Soviet Union 40
Caucasus 45

PART 2 INDIA

From India to Russia with Love 49
Maxim the Hare Krishna 52
Deconstructing Views 54
Visa Conundrums 57
Guruji 59
Youthful Developments 61
Seeking Confirmation 65
India and South Korea 68
Becoming a Yogi in India 73
Baba 76

PART 3 YOGA

Yoga and Lifestyle	89
Yoga as Paradox	92
A Worldly Yogi	94
Real and Fake Teachers	96
Karma	99
Culture	101
Interfaith Tantra Interview	103
Freedom and Discipline	105
The Correct Teachings	108
Appropriate Contexts	110
Spirit and Authenticity	113
Near Death Experience	117
Healing Myself	120

PART 4 A PLACE IN THE WORLD

Useless and Corrupt	127
Shiva and Shakti	129
Meditation and Respect	132
Resident Status	136
Yoga in Australia	137
Cultural Diversity	139
Australia and Globalization	142
Atheism and Dharma	147
Integrating Qualities	149
Jatis	152

CONTENTS

PART 5 TANTRA

Beyond Depression 157
Dharma and Anti-Dharma 160
Friendship 162
Krishnamurti 165
Trauma 167
Great Metaphors 169
Interfaith Tantra 171
Tantra and Yantra 177
Another View of Tantra 180
Choice and Practice 184
Jiva and Atman 189
Death and Life 191
Rabbit Holes and Fairytales 194
Emptiness 197
Spiritual Practice 198
Endings as Beginnings 200
Awakening 204

Epilogue 207

*The true Alchemist or Tantric
transforms mundane consciousness
into divine consciousness.*

Introduction

The moment I first set eyes on Yogi M an intuitive perception informed me that 'here was a special person'. Clad in the light desert orange of the Nath Yogic tradition, upright and emanating an aura of disciplined wisdom, he cut a fine figure. One immediately felt awed and humbled by his presence: and yet as an engaging conversation proceeded, I felt a simultaneous sense of warmth and ease.

The first encounter with Yogi was brief and held no suggestion of what was to unfold a year later. At the time Yogi was living in an Interfaith ashram in my home town of Warburton in the Upper Yarra Ranges of Victoria. Together with two of his Russian students and Nath practitioners, Yogi was a colourful addition to the local community. I knew nothing of Nath Yoga at the time.

How did someone born and raised in communist Soviet Union become a leader of Nath Yoga, one of India's oldest spiritual traditions? How did Yogi Matsyendranath become a resident in Australia? After-all, growing up in the atheistic environment of the Soviet Union wasn't exactly conducive to a deep interest and practice of any spiritual path. And Australia is a long way from Russia. I soon began to realise how unusual Yogi's life story was. Interspersed between his life in Russia and becoming a resident of Australia, there were years in other countries, mainly India and South Korea. Yogi is not only an authentic spiritual teacher but also a cosmopolitan citizen in the truest sense.

The web of inter-related events that lead to particular outcomes hints at hidden forces operating behind the screen of everydayness. It was so in the developing interaction between Yogi and myself. Yogi was a guest presenter at a fortnightly Interfaith gathering I co-facilitated with a local Benedictine monk and Catholic priest. Yogi's presentation and guided meditation was so potent and sublime and the story that he shared so intriguing that I mentioned afterwards to Yogi that someone ought to write his biography. When he agreed with my idea and later suggested I write it, an additional thread of the life-tapestry began its tentative first steps.

Henceforth, Yogi and I, and often one or two of his Nath students, met for recorded sessions, in conversations about his life, with me asking questions and Yogi responding. In this way Yogi, whose mysterious other-worldliness integrated with a charming human personality, became a fascinating part of my life. The impressive authenticity and gentle kindness of his character embedded themselves into my daily rhythms of working with him. He was always natural, easygoing and relaxed about how and when we would next meet and so we met as many times as felt necessary to capture the main features of his life story and teachings.

I'd never before worked on a draft in this way. There were many challenges in crafting a story in the first person, but on the other hand, the natural empathy I experienced with Yogi helped me to forge ahead with confidence. His aura of fine spiritual qualities never diminished. He was consistently conveying and manifesting authenticity, integrity, wisdom and compassion, and often a delightful childlike humour. His words were penetrating in their simplicity but he could also share difficult and

INTRODUCTION

subtle areas of teaching. Such an uprightness and noble persona did Yogi emanate that others often felt in awe of him. His presence naturally and without intention drew attention. Near the end of our time together, Yogi and his main student left Warburton and settled along the central coast of New South Wales. To complete the book I visited Yogi in New South Wales, and our friendship and collaboration deepened.

It isn't easy to describe the more subtle impressions Yogi makes, but on the last meet up with him in a Sydney cafe near Central Station, we exchanged views over a few hours, and this gave me ample time to observe him and reflect on those impressions. Even as he strode towards me in the station forecourt, a balance between an air of relaxed flow and upright centredness made him stand out from the crowd. He felt as an intimate friend but also not a friend one can possess. His natural meditative inwardness could be misconstrued as aloofness or even shyness, but I experienced it as an easy freedom, a way of being in the world but not quite of it, a sublime transmission that allows oneself to surrender to a natural pace. In this fashion we almost glided into a large cafeteria opposite the station and settled into a cosy corner area. Besides Yogi's pleasant demeanour and relaxed aura, there is also an intensity of focus when he is interested in a topic. And yet so softly spoken with a gentle cheerfulness. His penetrating blue eyes give a sense of being deeply interested in what one has to say. Not that we agreed on everything. But if Interfaith has taught me anything it is that there is room for difference within a framework that includes a singularity of love, the I Am awareness that sees through these eyes, hears through these ears and is s at-one-ment in its very nature.

We share a common interest in Interfaith and inter-spiritual dialogue. For a few years in Melbourne he shared accommodation with a Catholic Professor of Theology and a Buddhist Mahayana Lama. It was clear from the outset that Yogi was a flexible thinker with a depth of knowledge that transcended his own adopted Nath tradition.

This is not an ordinary biography. It is as much an inner story as an outer one. And someone who has an inner life as rich as Yogi does, naturally provides teachings through the telling of the outer biography. Yogi has dedicated his life to a deep and enthusiastic pursuit of the ancient path of Yoga and Tantra. Unlike many Western interpretations that trivialise these topics, Yogi presents a profound and illuminating journey through this mystical terrain.

The other unconventional feature is it being written in the first person, as if it were an autobiography. I didn't ghost write but rather crafted a book from numerous conversations. This style allows an immediacy and intimacy that a third person account would lack, in my opinion. The development of the text soon took on a dual nature: the biographical story and the teachings. These two threads interweave and complement each other and yet stand alone if the reader wants them to. Yogi's story is extraordinary and so are his teachings. This becomes apparent as the reader takes this journey, chapter by chapter. I am grateful to have been able to collaborate with Yogi Matsyendranath and render his important and fascinating story into English.

This book is dedicated to the spirit of open-minded spiritual research and practice. It is also an example of following one's heart. It is one person's story but in many ways our story too, ordinary and extraordinary at the same time.

Keith Simons

August 2017

PART 1

RUSSIA

*Supreme creativity arranges everything. You
only have to surrender to it.*

Beginnings

After a long cold winter and early spring, today is very pleasant. I leave the Interfaith ashram that is my temporary home and walk towards town. Everything feels different now. I have been granted a permanent resident visa status to stay in Australia. This is surreal and wonderful following many years of uncertainty.

Many have wanted to write my biography but it was not the right time or circumstances. It feels right now. A story of my life: why not? It is amazing, really. Some lives are especially unusual and represent something bigger, something about humanity, politics, social conditioning, spirituality and evolution that goes to the heart of what it means to be human.

How did a Russian become a yogi, living in the small rural town of Warburton in Victoria, Australia? How was Warburton hosting a Western leader of Nath Yoga? There will be many hows and whys in my story as it unfolds. It is a story spanning many lands and cultures. It is a story that I am ready to share.

I am talking to the writer of my story. We agree to meet as often as necessary for me to tell my story and he to craft it from my heavily accented and limited English into readable text.

We are mutually excited about this literary undertaking.

Where does a personal story begin? My belief is that a mystery is more than belief, and a story begins in a mystery that we are all a part of. This life and incarnation is like a bead on a chain. It is not random, so my birth in Russia was for a reason. It was not an accident.

I was born in Bryansk in 1976 near the Desna River, about three hundred and eighty kilometers south west of Moscow. The city is more historical than Moscow, existing for more than one thousand years. Here, twenty years of my life were lived. I will tell you a story of Bryansk and to begin with, a younger Yogi. Of course I was known by a different name back then.

At birth I was named Maxim. Maxim Zaharkin. Zaharkin has some historical lineage. Zechariah was derived from an Old Testament Hebrew prophet, traditionally considered to be the author of the Book of Zechariah. When I was twenty-eight, in India, a Sadhu gave me the name Yogi Matsyendranath but we shall talk more about that soon.

Others have wanted to write my biography, for example in Russia, and some Russian friends who had immigrated to the USA, but it was never a good time. Everything changed in 2015 when I received my permanent resident visa in Australia, so I am no longer a homeless refugee, no longer living with anxious uncertainty. Suddenly everything looks and feels different. I think my biographer can write a very good book. People in many countries would be interested in reading it.

In the meantime a few of my students and I are living in the Interfaith ashram in Warburton. We will meet for sessions of storytelling: a story of my life, a biography of a Russian Yogi.

Matsyendranath

It is mid-afternoon on a Sunday. My students and I have walked twenty-odd minutes from the ashram on the outskirts of town to the main street of Warburton. It is a delightful small town nestled on the banks of Victoria's principal river, the Yarra River. It is surrounded by mountains like a natural bowl protected by Gods and Goddesses, with the lifeblood of the Yarra flowing through it. For now I am very happy to be here.

It is a warm cloudy day and as we approach he is standing on the pavement. Seeing us he raises his arms and I do the same, like some secret occult greeting. We sit in the rear of his bookshop and begin.

"Beginning of a long journey", he says. "I will ask a few questions to get us into the mood. You were born Maxim Zaharkin?"

I tell him this was my normal name. I received a renewed passport when twenty-eight with a new spiritual name.

A new spiritual name can change your destiny. It brings in a different energy. Life can change according to your view and a name change can alter the view.

I received my name Matsyendranath in India from a Sadhu and my Guru sanctioned it later. It is a very famous name in Tantra. The word, *matsya* in Sanskrit means fish and I was born in the sign of Pisces. *Indra* is King in Vedic symbolism, so it could mean the King of Fishes: King Fish. And *nath* means master. I had to laugh at the sound of King Fish. Words can be experienced as humorous when not your first language.

"But Nath is also the name of the yoga you practice?"

Yes. There is a mythic story here. Matsyendranath was a fisherman. A fish swallowed Matsyendranath and when in the stomach of the fish, it came to the bank of an ocean, where Shiva and Shakti sat close by in discussion. Shiva was trying to give secret knowledge of Tantric Yoga to Shakti, but Shakti was tired and slept. Shiva asked, 'Are you listening?' but she was sleeping. Matsyendranath, who was in the belly of the fish said, 'I am listening.' Shiva recognized there was a person inside the fish and said, 'Okay, if you listen I'll give you this knowledge.' After that Shakti, wife of Shiva, awoke and understanding what was happening became angry. Shakti said to Matsyendranath, 'I will curse you and therefore you must worship me all your life.' After a while Matsyendranath came out of the fish's stomach and became a famous Tantric and Yogi who transmitted this knowledge to his disciple Gorakhnath. Gorakhnath is the founder of the Nath tradition. He is very famous in India. This is a classic story.

Keith listens with a genuine expression of interest and asks, "So this story relates strongly to your name? Was this name given because you are a Piscean and also because you were a good listener and student like the original Matsyendranath?"

Yes, this is why; it is a part of the significance. I think so.

Indeed as I was to discover, Keith has an expansive interest in world faiths. Now he has a new mythic story to add to his collection.

Maxim the Artist

Nowadays Russia tries to be religious but in that time religion was considered crazy.

I was born in 1976. It was the Soviet Union and in the midst of the cold war. So-called super powers viewed each other with almost paranoid suspicion. The Soviet Union was like an island cast off from the Western world, floating in an ideology that weaved its influence into all corners of society: into every aspect of people's lives.

Like everyone else my parents were under the influence of communism. I don't know how sincerely they supported communism but every respected person in society had to believe or at least pretend to, or they were somehow perceived as enemies of the motherland. My parents had influence but it's difficult to say how seriously they believed. In a society like the Soviet Union it was difficult to express one's innermost thoughts. Free speech was not an option unless one was prepared to risk much.

My father was the vice-director of a large building company. He had reasons to not say anything too controversial. President Putin awarded my mother special recognition for services to society. She contributed much to Russia and was respected. Putin gave her official status and acknowledgement.

I have one sister, Tatiana, a year younger than me. She married a very educated Turk who was interested and knowledgeable about world religions. We had some interesting conversations. He is multi-lingual too. He arranged meetings for me with some Sufis.

A few Turks lived and conducted business in Bryansk. They were involved in construction, especially new buildings, and my father was connected to some of them. My brother-in-law was the owner of a construction company and he and my father had a business relationship.

Tatiana is more interested nowadays in spiritual matters, but not so much back then. Ironically she gave me a spiritual book as a birthday present when we were both quite young. It was a book about Vajrayana or Tantric Buddhism. She must have naturally intuited my interest. I think I was younger than twelve. I've always had a good relationship with my sister. Maybe the book was a portent.

When I returned to Russia from India years later to renew my visa I gave my mother a mantra for her health condition and she started to practice. I believe my mother had some inherent intuition but nowadays it is more developed.

My father was mostly absent: he was very busy, always working. He had many meetings with people and his big title matched his confidence. He was much in demand. This created some conflict within the family. My parents would have arguments but now it is fine. They are still living and working in Bryansk. We speak by phone sometimes, but not often.

From an early age I became independent. To begin with they supported me. They eventually gave me an apartment where I lived alone, in

Bryansk, close to an art college where I studied, hoping to be an artist in the future. I studied various forms of art: landscape, portrait, and industrial design.

From childhood I felt a type of beauty behind things, like another dimension, but it was indescribable. So what is there? I hadn't much information about a supreme energy, being or beauty, but I felt it. I tried to express through my paintings an expression of '*That*'.

A student says, "When I came to his classes he expressed that he'd lost interest in painting because it couldn't really express this beauty as it is. That some limitation is present in human expression, and in his."

I felt this presence everywhere. I thought how can an artist such as I express this with excellence and brilliance?

Keith says, "I heard recently that artists always feel some discontent. There is a tension. A striving that is never fully satisfied."

This is correct. Always trying to express something that is out of reach: this was a like a pure but unattainable vision. I think supreme beauty and supreme Shakti always pursue me, in all of my activities. It is indescribable, but how can one express this? Maybe to live it or be it is closer than any description: closer to the reality.

Maybe in my youth the closest I came to describing 'That' was by the words 'supreme beauty' and 'grace' or something like that. I felt it more strongly when I began to practice Qigong and Yoga and had more of a real experience. Then appeared a dilemma: what should I do; art or dedicate my whole life to Yoga?

Sometimes you perceive a veil and behind it are hints of reality, but it is not complete. I felt to do art, but when I started to practice Qigong and Yoga the veil slowly, increasingly, evaporated like mist.

These practices are more internal than art. You can connect easily to this beauty and are not separate from it. Whereas in art you are a little bit separate. Art tries to express the inexpressible whereas inner practices feel it. The gulf between being and doing closes.

I will tell you a good example about art. In art I sometimes could feel tension. This happened once when somebody ordered a picture from me, and I painted for money: immediately realizing something from an interesting perspective this situation catalyzed. An insight and awakening occurred. Right then and there I made a decision.

I would do some paintings for pleasure, for my heart, and others for selling. This was a compromise between the world and me, but it didn't entirely remove the tension. A disturbed feeling remained.

Another time my mother invited some of her friends home who were interested in buying some of my paintings. When those people came to my home they looked at all of my paintings and they asked, 'Can we buy this or that painting?'

I said, 'No, that is my own,' and they said, 'We will pay you more.' They continued to raise the price and continued to visit, many times, always increasing their bid. They thought they could change my mind. It brought me to a deep, sincere, awareness of what I should do.

In that time there was no problem existing with both money and self-realization: no conflict as such. I understood if I gave myself to the pursuit of money I could lose everything. I could lose the money and lose self-realization, so therefore it was understood: *it is especially important to discover one's mission in life.*

Even within art I realized my spiritual mission, because spirituality was related to my real Self. Therefore I regarded art as inseparable from spiritual living.

This was all happening when I was between eighteen and twenty. I felt this creative energy as Shakti and that it was unlimited. You can work and work and never find it. I had found it and was determined to not just throw it away, or sell it to the demon of money or fame.

I was surprised that some people in Russia were jealous of me. They witnessed something that made me attractive to people, like a magnet. They didn't understand what was happening or why. Some thought it must be a trick, like cultivating charisma, or some secret formula I'd mastered. They didn't understand or perceive that Shakti was not personal.

I have done many jobs in my life but never cared about recognition. When you are doing something enjoyable there is an abundance of energy. It is Shakti acting through the personal self.

Those who don't understand think, 'Oh you think so much about your career.' Because many people had lost their way it was difficult to understand. In this way my vocation happened spontaneously. Supreme creativity arranges everything. You only have to surrender to it. It is not about seeking attention. It is a natural surrendering and deep enjoyment.

Even then I understood this.

Shifting Sands

The kitchen is an old colonial style, large and comfortable. We sit around a wooden table and wait for the tea to be poured.

I believe it is possible to create a beautiful book.

"Beautiful and interesting. Maybe if we can combine beauty and interest then a good book can happen. There are many interesting biographies written but to my mind they lack spiritual depth. I might enjoy reading a book like that but at the conclusion feel dissatisfied. The type of book I would most like to write is the type of book I'd most like to read. I believe with your story Yogi an excellent book can be crafted that is both beautiful and interesting; it is possible."

My student sips her tea. "A bitter and sweet experience: not necessarily the normal, for instance some may express spiritual things in a beautiful picturesque way, without the real situation being revealed: too polished. Do you know what I mean?"

"The lotus without the mud," Keith offers a metaphor.

Always one strives for credibility but credibility and beauty are related. Some bad things have happened in my life, but when faced are always related to other experiences. Everything is related. Nothing bad was fatal because I overcame problems. So a biography should be an honest account: the good, bad, ugly and beautiful. Then even the bad and the ugly can be beautiful. I can also share my point of view. How do human beings overcome adversity?

"Wasn't overcoming a major part of your story?" asks Keith.

Yes, of course. It hasn't been an easy journey. In Russia some people became conflicted because of the State or other powers. They sacrificed something. These powers come between and interfere. So it is a great opportunity to discover renunciation in oneself. Renunciation of any size and shape can be a way to grow. For instance, between Russia and Western society there is conflict and this doesn't make for a healthy atmosphere for many. Sometimes people lose touch with compassion and humane feelings. I understand, but it is difficult to overcome, this conflicted atmosphere.

"Were you aware of this conflict as a child?"

We all experienced it. I felt it even in my childhood but also felt something supreme everywhere, and had a lot of questions. Those who were much older than me couldn't or wouldn't answer many of my questions, or at least not to my satisfaction. For example I asked my history teacher, 'How should one conform to changing political views. One time Stalin is great. Then he is bad dictator.' The teacher said, 'You, Maxim are not an expert in these matters. It is not good for you to have doubts.' He was pulling rank in order to gag me, trying to suppress my desire to know the truth.

When people ask such questions there is something the teachers or others understand but keep silent about. Of course, they cannot acknowledge it officially. I kept asking questions in different ways, to teachers, parents and others. My parents had good social positions and more or less played along party lines. I didn't get much information from them.

During my childhood I heard mostly criticism of religion and churches. It was more general criticism rather than particular details. I partly agreed with these criticisms because I realized churches had destructive energies. Hidden subtly, churches were involved in politics, but behind this there was also something pure. I felt that too. After so many years there were some mystical traditions that were essential and pure. Even though there was some truth in the social criticisms there was also something good. I had this feeling but no one could validate it or confirm it for me.

"Were you lonely at this time?"

Something very interesting was happening. I was comfortable being alone and the more alone I was, the more people came to my house. People wanted to have discussions. At first, when I was in Art College, I started practicing Yoga. I was about eighteen. Then people became interested and attracted to me. Yoga brought me a lot of energy, supreme energy. I felt it everywhere. There were a few people who felt a deeper connection to me and the first students joined my first real Yoga group. I had started teaching Yoga before that but not with a group.

My student adds, 'I was sixteen and in my last year of school. I saw an advertisement for Yoga and so I joined his first group. He was only eighteen.'

Actually I didn't intend to teach Yoga. It just happened. Nowadays people have some certificate or open a center. I became a Yoga teacher without any expectation that this would happen. When I was eleven I began to learn martial arts and now at eighteen I was a Yoga teacher.

Childhood

Boys were tough in Russia. How can I explain this? There was a lot of bullying: on the streets, everywhere, so I sought protection, some kind of self-defense. I wasn't aggressive but I needed protection. I have never been an aggressive person but there were a lot of rascals. In many cities in Russia there were gangs, very organized, like a youth mafia.

In Russian they are called *contora*: I find this interesting but not easy to explain. It is like an imitation of Government but with criminal minds and intentions.

There is another word that means something like registration. The word *propiska* means something like that, registration to join and belong to a regional gang. The leaders would ask, 'Who do you know? What contacts do you have?' It is complicated, but across Russian cities there is this criminal atmosphere.

When the Soviet Union collapsed in about 1991, these criminal activities became commonplace. It was dreadful, and a shadow of normal life, like the law of the jungle. It became very dangerous from 1991. From the 1990's to 2000 it was serious, especially for children. I think most boys during this time practiced some form of martial arts. My own involvement then, when I was eleven and older, was complex.

I was a black sheep in my family. I felt like a black sheep, but think it was good because it saved me from a bad fate. For instance, it is a big mistake to focus mainly on money. My cousin died because of this. He wasn't doing anything at the time but he was killed suddenly. Others died who learnt martial arts and became involved in criminal activities, including friends. I thought, 'I must be aware of this situation.'

My martial arts teacher provided a future for boys to become criminals, not intentionally, but in effect that was what it led them to. I don't think he really had a spiritual understanding or interest. It was like helping to create jobs in which you could earn money quickly, but many of those boys died before long. It was a brutal way of surviving. Everything was dangerous. This was the environment of my youth. It was difficult to even survive intact, and to not get entangled in those criminal webs. It was a very, very bad time in Russia, and there was a lot of abuse against girls too, rape and violence.

Many clever people understood martial arts only in the physical aspect, without any appreciation of a mystical or spiritual dimension. It was all about fighting and surviving, or about criminal business and who was controlling whom. My teacher had a little understanding that there was a deeper level to martial arts, but at that time in Russia spirituality was considered irrelevant and unhelpful. It was thought that one should only react quickly, injure those who stood in your way without thinking, and in this way survive.

I think my teacher did sometimes briefly ponder about the Eastern spirituality behind martial arts, but he considered martial arts more in the sense of being a warrior, for succeeding in daily situations. I think personally this was a big mistake, because even if you are a very skilled warrior with quick reactions, you are never quicker than bullets. Plus what happens to oneself also depends on an understanding of life. Therefore I believe I am very lucky to have avoided fatal situations.

Keith is listening with fascination. "Were you ever tempted?"

I think so, but always reasoned with myself. Yes, they tried to tempt me to do particular things. They would say, 'You can earn good money.'

Keith thinks this is like grooming. How people can be 'groomed' into criminal or abusive circumstances and roles.

Yes, they tried to groom me. I think a lot about this. A mature way of thinking was always within me. When I was very young my grandfather who was Russian but born in the Caucasus area, from my mother's lineage, said, 'Everyone should die and enter into another dimension.'

I was very young and had never heard about death. I asked him, 'What is another dimension? What does it mean to die?' He found it difficult to explain. I discovered within though something like feelings of immortality. I tried to describe it to him but I think he didn't understand what I was talking about. He had heard something about another dimension, and of course he witnessed people dying.

When I first saw a corpse I thought, 'There is something else there, something behind the corpse,' but it was indescribable. After that, when I listened to my grandfather speaking about religion I felt warmth and connection, especially towards my grandmother, who was a genuinely religious person. *Babushka* and *Dedushka* in Russian, were my dear grandparents. I felt this special something in my childhood but I believe it was in my nature, something beyond hereditary.

I remember my birth too, in some strange way. When my mother described my difficult birth, and doctors made some mistakes, I felt a confirmation. I don't know what kind of memory this is. You know sometimes there are memories that are like archetypes. In this way I think I have a memory of the process of my birth. My mother was surprised. How I could know that? This type of memory is supersensible.

"Does this type of supersensible memory extend to before your birth?"

I think I remember. You know memory is not a simple subject. For example, right now I am talking to you and you listen to me, but there are other thoughts in the periphery of my awareness, other sensory experiences. So in this present moment we talk and my sensory awareness is focused on you, but also in this moment, other things are happening, and yet in the future I will only remember talking to you. In this way I am not completely aware of past situations.

It is possible to increase awareness. For me, it is not like how people generally describe past incarnations. I have a different sense of this. I believe it was my choice to be born in Russia. I brought some good to Russia, for the people there, from India back to Russia. I have spoken about many bad things in Russia but there are also many deep, good things, because this country has absorbed much Eastern culture as well as Western. There is something very special there, something in Russia that you cannot find in Western society.

Keith wonders about a Russian author who wrote a series of books about Russia claiming that a long time ago Russia was known as Kievan Rus, a type of empire with Kiev as capital or center. Russian pagans lived on the territories of Russia with cults very similar to the Indo-Aryan, and that this knowledge has been suppressed in Russian history. Actually Christianity suppressed it. The old knowledge survived until the thirteenth century and some old orthodox churches in Russia assimilated and accepted some influences from those old Pagan, religious times.

You can find many beautiful things in these threads, names of deities and you know many Russian words are similar to Sanskrit. Some tribes travelled between India and Russia and exchanged their religious cultures, maybe some gypsies from Rajasthan also. So many words in Sanskrit and Russian have the same roots, and some words are completely the same. There is definitely a relationship. It was a two-way exchange I think.

My student concurs. "Yes, for example, many rivers in Russia have names similar to Sanskrit words. One River is *Moksha* which is the Sanskrit word meaning liberation."

But fortunately or unfortunately, when Christianity came to Russia much of the old knowledge was lost, knowledge from the thirteenth century and beyond.

"The author also claims that the Christians with Vladimir the Great (a prince of Novgorod) came and destroyed much of the existing folk culture. It seems that Kievan Rus was more a people than a country, and this consciousness was like Indigenous thinking, very close to the land and inherently spiritual in a natural way."

Some people in Russia have researched and reviewed this, but because the evidence was destroyed it's difficult to have precise information. You know in those times there were not separate countries, like Russia, Ukraine and so on. Many people are talking about the connection with Indo-Aryan these days. There are differences of opinion but I think everyone agrees there is a relationship with Indian culture, but the question is what kind of relationship?

In those times, national borders did not restrict people as now. There was no need for visas. Now in Russia every scientist and political person rewrites history to serve a limited self-interest. Therefore I am very careful in taking a definite stand. For instance Ukrainian and Russian historians argue from their own national perspectives, even about the superiority of the language. Of course there were many small kingdoms then, but no strict borders separating people. Kiev was known as Kievan Rus and was the center of Rus culture. Over time each group had their own interests, a type of tribalism developed and this created a lot of problems, like the story of the Tower of Babel.

Bryansk

In Bryansk there was an old, historic Christian monastery that was mostly destroyed by Soviet forces, by Bolsheviks. It was called Svensky Monastery. There was a famous monk and warrior, Peresvet, who was a meaningful part of Russian history. He fought another warrior and they killed each other at the same moment. Now at that site, there is a strong energy.

Bryansk is also famous for the partisans who fought the Nazis during the time of German occupation, between 1941 and 1943. They created a lot of problems for the Germans. There are many dense forests around Bryansk and the partisans could hide and make sudden attacks and ambushes. In these forests there were also many Pagan people practicing magic, like witchcraft.

The word *Bryansk* means something like dense bush. *Debryansk* is an old Russian name and *debr* means a valley covered with dense forest and bushes. It is difficult to walk through and you can easily lose your bearings and become lost, maybe like the lowlands or valley from which it derives its name. Major rivers, like the Dnieper and Desna, join and then find their way to the Black Sea, and ships sailed on these rivers. Bryansk was therefore a major river port. In olden times the Desna was very wide and there were many ships.

Bryansk is beside a hill and a fortress overlooks the town. My grandparents lived through those years of occupation and shared stories about hiding from the bombing and being afraid.

"I too was born and lived in Bryansk," adds my student, "and I can say that everyone in Bryansk felt motivated to try and escape from there."

Yes, there was a big motivation to escape. This was especially true from 1991 when the Soviet Union collapsed. Before that it was so-so. When the Soviet Union collapsed all manner of criminal things started. From then on we wanted to escape. Officially, Russian authorities said now the Soviet Union is finished, democracy is here, no more corruption. But actually it became more corrupt and criminal.

You know sometimes challenging situations are positive for personal development, for greater awareness.

Now is a good time to tell my story because with residency in Australia life has seriously changed. It is a good time to try and describe my life up to now. Many people will want to read such a book, even in Russia. But we must describe my life very honestly. My biography can help people everywhere understand what Russia is.

You know, I immigrated because there is something I don't like about Russia, but also there is something I like, and it is the same for Western culture. Therefore I want to be neutral in that way and be very honest. It is important for us that a book is written in English. This can be beautiful and interesting.

No one has become a Russian yogi in the Nath tradition before. In America and Europe, there are many yogis. But how in a communist country like Russia can someone become a yogi? So a biography can be wise and deep. For me it is enjoyable to remember but even in the life before Yoga there is interest. Uninteresting is also interesting.

Even grey has a story. Even grey can be represented and described. My students were seeking something. Within the grey some impulse was there, so grey can be beautiful too.

"In Bryansk I studied with Yogi, and slowly layer by layer was removed. And then I became a real seeker. I became motivated and my consciousness became wider."

Birth Trauma

As for my birth I almost strangled on the umbilical cord. They had to cut my mother, but I have mostly wiped this memory from my subconscious. It was a natural birth and I almost died. My mother was okay but they had to prevent strangulation, something like that. The doctors were afraid there might be a bad outcome, but at the last moment they did something, and I lived.

Maybe there were some later health problems relating to this birth trauma but Yoga helped to heal them. Even early in my childhood when I practiced martial arts my health improved. I strengthened my immune system and capacity to survive. In life there can be disturbances, but if there is an inner soul fire you can change many bodily things. I think almost all diseases or defects can be changed.

Nowadays modern science, including medicine, accepts that they don't know all solutions, but they think in the future we shall discover them, but really they are accepting they don't know. So is it possible to solve or not?

In our nature we have capacities for self-healing that are commonly unknown. In regards to the birth trauma I had some problems, with lungs, kidneys and so on, but these problems were healed in time.

Black Sheep

The term *black sheep* can have many interpretations. For some being a black sheep is a rejection of what is perceived as normality, but for others it is an inherent and natural quality of being, a natural and unforced quality that stands out as different to the social norm. I believe I am the latter type of black sheep.

I felt that within this human life there is an invisible dimension that is omnipresent and broad, that helps to guide and create one's destiny, and that this is knowable even if most don't know it. People identify with passing moods like sadness, or they have a fatalistic attitude. For instance, that one cannot change, that all is fated and fixed like a spiritual prison. There are some people who think a spiritual prison, or any prison, is not so bad. They accept it. But I am not a revolutionary type of black sheep. It is simply my nature to be as I am.

When I was very young I think some realized I was different to the norm in some way. Definitely my mother. She was aware that I was resistant and unaccepting of many of their expectations. I rebelled against many of my parent's standard views. Then much later they said, "It is better if you live alone," and gave me an apartment. They thought, 'Maxim can arrange his life according to his own feelings.' They didn't avoid their parental responsibility but rather realized how independent I was.

There were a few teachers who perceived me as different, in a positive way too. An example of my independent thinking was when people generally read a book about Lenin or wrote an essay about him and they tended to conform in their views" 'Yes, Lenin is a genius.' Teachers also conformed to a general consensus but I thought, 'Teachers can be quite stupid too.' Well, maybe not so much stupid, more like primitive; you know, they go to work, pick up their wages and repeat views like a common script without questioning or thinking. They don't like to make waves or invite trouble. They don't really care about the children in their care. But a few teachers were good.

One, a woman, was my main class teacher. She was very creative and interested in studying life, and it was she who understood something about me, that somehow I was special among her students, and it was she who organized an exhibition of my paintings. She was a general teacher but also a musician and appreciator of art. We had discussions about art and life.

I actually had many friendships and felt friendship was the most important priority in life. This felt like a natural part of who I was and I always supported my friends if I could. For example in my art class I helped others; sometimes I helped the whole class as if I was the assistant teacher. My teacher gave me extra tasks and even at times left me in charge if she needed to go somewhere. I would draw for my friends, sometimes for the whole class. These students helped me in other ways, with subjects like mathematics that I would copy from them. In this way I experienced positive exchanges and mutual respect, even if somewhat cagey and underhand because the teacher wasn't present.

Collapse of the Soviet Union

When the Soviet Union collapsed I was close to fifteen. We students didn't really understand what was happening. The majority of people were not aware of what really happened. Gorbachev used words like *perestroika* and I listened and thought 'What is he talking about?' No one really understood his views. He talked about freedom and independence. That was good in that Russia became an open society, but we were not aware of what kind of capacity for openness was present.

I think for some people who had a criminal type of mind, they saw an opportunity. They could use this new situation for their own advantage: to have power over others who were less able to use this changed situation. Some could become millionaires, billionaires, because there was more freedom now. The entire situation was unstable. The atmosphere was chaotic. Some understood law and now could use it to their advantage, but the majority of people were unaware. It is always like this. When some people are rich then others are poor.

So it was a good thing that Russia became open and many people could travel more easily than before, but if you were poor, how could you travel in this new open society? Western countries made it difficult to obtain visas. Therefore there was a big illusion, a fantasy about freedom that many people had. Maybe for Westerners who had never stayed in

Russia, it seemed that Gorbachev had only a good impact. I am not saying it was either good or bad. It was just that in this new Russia there were many problems as well.

There were wars happening, Chechnya for instance, and Tajikistan with its many refugees. That country has become even poorer than Russia. Many escaped and came to Moscow. A new chaos replaced the old one, with more freedom, but alongside it increased criminality. I didn't have much understanding then as a fourteen year old but my parents and other older people understood a lot. Younger people were not really aware of what had happened and was happening.

This new wave of *contora* or criminal activity that existed before the collapse of the Soviet Union became stronger and in a way it became more than contora. It was a more serious type of criminal activity. People already had guns. In Russian there is a word, *roof* which is like a criminal protection racket. Some person attacks you and then someone comes to your business and says 'Can I help you? You have a problem and I can fix it for you: offer you protection. But you must pay me some money.'

This was forced manipulation. If you said I have no money to pay you, you could be in big trouble. Many business people were killed or had not so mysterious accidents. For example a car stops and someone shoots. Or someone would enter your shop and ask, 'So how much can you pay us?' And you say 'I am very poor. I have a small business'. And they say something like, 'Yes you have a small business but it is better than no business. You could have no business.'

These criminal gangs used some young men and boys, and even young boys often tried to imitate these actions, these roles. Films depicted these characters so they became as super heroes. Some of these criminals had spent time in prison and had their own special signs and ways of relating, a bit like in freemasonry. It is called *fenya* in Russian slang, which means to speak in thieves slang. They created this *fenya*, slang, especially to communicate in prison, so police or prison guards could not understand what was spoken. This became a sub-culture and then became a general criminal atmosphere in society.

If you were called certain words it was very, very, bad news. For example 'rooster' had particular derogatory connotations and expectations that one would respond in a certain way. If certain words were used towards you and you didn't respond in the correct way, or didn't respond at all, it could become a big problem. This communication therefore had an expectation that was prescribed, like a fixed set of rules, a coded way to control people. This became more evident when I was close to finishing school. It began maybe even when I was thirteen. I already heard about these things. Even in our school there were two brothers from a criminal family who had prison experiences. One brother explained many things about these criminal occult-type customs.

Many girls were attracted to this macho image with its possibility of being with rich men, and even the glamour of being with criminals. Because being rich and being a criminal went together in that time, when Perestroika began. They were very crazy times.

There is the mafia in Italy, but I think in Russia it was much worse. Some had special tattoos with special meanings. In Russian prisons there was a type of caste system. Some performed coronation ceremonies as if they were Kings or Emperors. There were those who were controlling this criminal structure, keeping it going. There is a term 'thief within the law', that is similar to saying legal thievery. A sort of criminal government created by police in the Soviet Union that then migrated to the prisons, because they wanted some order within the prison system. Order within the criminal society is understandable, so it became like a de-facto system allowed by the state.

In Russia hierarchy was believed to be crucial. When the police arrested such a 'legal thief' and indicated a crime, he could not deny his status. He would have to honestly say that he is a thief within the law. If he hid this fact, he would be killed by someone from his 'fraternity'. If police prevented a criminal leader from operating then he couldn't claim his status within the hierarchy. So they had these 'codes of conduct'. Then everybody knew their positions in the network.

Interestingly, these concepts spread to general life. It was like an extension of prison life. There are many versions of how this happened. Many people think Stalin created this criminal structure because there were many political prisoners in his era. After the Russian revolution many people didn't approve of the changed situation and ended up in prison or were sent to Siberia. It was a change in lifestyle and many didn't like that. Stalin said, 'Okay you can arrange your own affairs but it will be legal only for your community.' It wasn't only the police who perpetrated this hidden, shadowy dimension, but the ruling elite too. It was actually Stalin who initiated it. He literally created a class of legal criminality in Russia under the guise of servants of the law. So you could be a leader in prison or a leader of criminals out of prison.

Personally I was very aware to not be involved in any of this. Many boys were attracted to it, and felt it was interesting and alluring. They created romantic images. Every boy wanted to be respected but a lot of questions arose in my mind. Why does one think that this society is independent and open when the police arrange these activities and perpetrate this hidden, shadowy dimension? This was not the independence that many people sought, including me.

With Gorbachev only the surface external shape changed but essentially it was the same. You can say nowadays there is a democracy. I think Russia never had democracy in its entire history. There were the Tsars before the communists but Russia never had democracy. Somehow I understood that real change was impossible and this was unacceptable for me.

Many people wanted to get out of Russia, especially in the villages and small towns, because there was no positive hope for the future, for a better life. People were poor and engaged in little activity. It was all just about surviving. At the same time after Perestroika, the Government stole money from the national budget. Of course these things are complex and difficult to describe. Workers in factories were not paid salaries for months or even longer. Can you imagine working for a year and not getting paid? How could people survive in those conditions? Workers were paid by being given products that they were producing. Some products you had helped to create and then would have to try and sell. People somehow survived. It was a difficult time and survival became the main focus. Some people had a garden or plot of land and could grow some vegetables.

After Gorbachev there was a lot of human suffering. People couldn't easily immigrate to other countries because the embassies said, 'Ah you want to be a refugee. You have a democratic country here; isn't this good enough?' I think that people didn't understand what type of democracy they had. If they had opened the borders everyone would have escaped. I am exaggerating a bit but you get the point. There was a lot of dissatisfaction.

In earlier times if I wanted to travel to another country I needed to get permission to leave from Russian authorities, then permission to get a passport, and only after that could I apply for a visa. It was a very difficult bureaucratic process in the time of the Soviet Union. It was a bit similar to North Korea. So it was not easy to leave Russia.

There were some good results after the demise of the Soviet Union. We must thank Gorbachev for some changes and bureaucratic structures which were relaxed and simplified, but it was not all roses.

Caucasus

Before I was eleven years of age, art was my favorite subject at school. Even when I was very young I made soldiers from bread, like dough sculptures, or by using mud, making pictures. Some children had more of an interest in the sciences and others in what you call here, humanities. I veered strongly towards the humanities, the arts.

For periods during my childhood I lived in the Caucasus area, in the mountains. That was my mother's region. There were some Russian enclaves there. They had been sent there because they had rejected external rites of the church, refused to perform military service and take an oath. They had their own type of religious orthodoxy.

In 1841 Nicholas the first, emperor of Russia, had sent such Russians to the Caucasus area. In this environment, Georgia and surrounds in the time of the Soviet Union had no border between Armenia and Georgia. A few Russian villages were established in that time, maybe five or six and Russians lived harmoniously with the native Georgians and Armenians. They stayed apart but traded with each other.

So this was also a part of my childhood. I was given a job as a shepherd, tending to sheep and cows and working in the fields. I would often sit and look at the mountains. It was a way to enjoy the beauty of nature. I was very young but these experiences made a positive impression.

My father was from Bryansk but spent time in Caucasus, and I did too before starting school and sometimes afterwards. The native Caucasians are a different type of people. They are very natural. They have their own religiosity and customs. They dress and eat differently to Russians and have a folk culture with unique ways of agriculture. They are less sophisticated and I loved this simplicity.

PART 2

INDIA

You know, if you see beauty that is indescribable you understand it is everywhere, in every movement, totally alive ...

From India to Russia with Love

When I last visited Russia, two years ago, I didn't have permanent residency here in Australia, therefore I felt differently to now. It was like entering and merging into another dimension, completely different. When I re-entered Russia everything from before disappeared.

I had invited my *Guruji*, (Guruji is a term of endearment for one's Guru in the Indian spiritual tradition), to come to Russia with me, which was a rare occurrence. He was from Nepal but came to Bryansk with me and was happy to be there. It was unusual for Bryansk to be visited by someone like this. Many schools in his own country adored him. He was the Guru of the King of Nepal. We didn't advertise his visit to Russia. We only informed my students because I thought it was best to only arrange meetings with those who in my mind were honest, respectful and interested.

I brought something to Russia that was new for this country. I believe therefore I did much good for Russia. I wanted a Russia where one religion didn't dominate, and where religion wasn't artificial.

It is not good if you only have grey color, it becomes boring. In Russia there was not much religious diversity. Under those circumstances the real intelligence of people slowly, slowly, evaporates.

Of course America was depicted as the enemy and we were expected to do everything against them, but my view was Russians ought to study and research the strong positive things about America, Europe and other countries, including India. There are good and bad things in every country. I wished for positive developments in Russia and wanted to see people become intelligent and culturally aware. They already had some culture but it was not very broad. It was in my mind when leaving Russia that I should discover something worthy of bringing back.

You know, every culture has good and bad features. I could see there were good things in Western society and in Russia, and also bad features. For instance, in Western societies there is often plenty of everything, but much that is superficial and artificial. Spirituality can be that way too: the New Age movement has much that is superficial, like spiritual McDonalds or Coca Cola.

Sometimes when you have over-eaten it is because there is too much food, easily available. In this way spirituality can become like a supermarket. In Russia, because for many years we were a closed country we actually had more of an open mind for anything new. New things had more of an impact because there was a certain hunger, a sincere desire to explore everything. There was curiosity because we hadn't been able to really discover what was out there beyond our borders.

When I came to India I met many sincere people who wanted to sacrifice their lives to explore their traditions, and you can find some people in Russia who also sincerely want to explore deeply, including Indian spirituality. Not many perhaps because when people began to understand about spiritual matters they realized it was not so easy. They dipped their toes in the ocean and then walked away, sometimes very promptly.

In the time of the Soviet Union I had bought some books on the black market and they inspired an appetite. You know sometimes a black market is not so bad. These books were certainly one link that led me to India.

I first went to India when I was little older than twenty and arrived without money. Most Gurus in India are interested in money. I am not judging this, only stating a fact. Good and bad depend on the situation and context, and there are many rogues in India.

When I came to India I knew nothing about the country. In Russia there was no internet, no accurate descriptions of other countries. This was to be a great new adventure, one that was to have profound and sublime influences. So it was with some Indian experience that I returned to Russia with Guruji with interesting stories to share.

Maxim the Hare Krishna

In Russia I had a Ukrainian teacher. I was his student for a short time but when in 1998 there was a big economic crisis in Russia and Ukraine, he immigrated to the USA. I thought: I cannot immigrate to the USA without money; that would be too difficult. So where could I go?

I had already dreamt about going to India. I'd heard many beautiful things about India and thought it would be very interesting to go there.

I came across someone who belonged to the Hare Krishna mission. He didn't work. In the time of Communism he'd been in prison because he didn't follow Marxist-Leninist ideology. They thought of such people as American provocateurs who try to corrupt communist ideology, as if it was an imperialist religion that destroys our communist culture. When they released him no one would employ him. So he asked for donations, in shops and on the streets. After he was freed from prison I met him.

Before that I visited Cyprus. I wanted to earn money to go to India, but I didn't find any jobs. It was very difficult to find a legal job at that time. I met this Hare Krishna guy at the airport. I was very surprised. I'd met him many years before. He said, 'We could meet in Moscow'. He gave me his phone number. 'Please call us.'

I caught a different plane to him, another flight, and I came to Moscow. My intention was to find a job there. I had been promised work in Moscow but it never happened. Nothing was provided for me. They said I could work as a Yoga teacher via an employment agency, but they were empty promises. They had a fitness center and it could have included Yoga, but it didn't happen, so I called this Krishna guy and rented a room in a hotel. He said his ashram was close to my hotel, only a hundred meters away. I saw this as a significant sign and that I should visit him.

When I came to the ashram he explained his story and I told him about my failed job here in Moscow and that I wanted to go to India. He said, 'I can help you go to India, no need to work to get the money. Don't believe those who tell you otherwise. No one can help you in life; you must use a spiritual way like me. Make the spiritual way the priority; it will solve any problem. First you must remove spiritual problems, immediately'.

He taught me how to collect donations in market places. Every day I witnessed hundreds of people who had studied and had degrees but were jobless or found mundane jobs, maybe in markets. I finally collected enough money to purchase a one-way ticket to India. Even the airline didn't like to sell me the ticket but finally I convinced them that I had friends in India and they would buy me a return ticket and provide for me. They relented and I had my ticket. My Hare Krishna friend had told me that in India everyone would donate money. It would be easy to survive like that.

Deconstructing Views

I tried to live like a Sannyasin in India but it was difficult. This became my lifestyle, travelling to many places. For example, I would arrive in a city and collect money, some for food, sometimes for a cheap hotel. I was very independent, and would spend a few days somewhere and then move onto another place. For about a half year in Moscow I'd already lived a bit like that, and now in India. I would approach people and tell them that I lived like a monk and that according to our religion we didn't work, so can you donate some money, according to your capacity. Some people donated towards visiting sacred places, visiting ashrams and so on. My introduction was simple. I would introduce myself and in one or two sentences explain. I did consider myself a Hare Krishna follower to some extent at that time. I felt I'd belonged to the Krishna movement in Moscow especially because other religions from India were hardly known about in Russia at that time.

I learnt many stories from them and was sincere about it. I was really interested to learn their doctrine, but was more interested in Yoga. Yoga is not a strong element in the Hare Krishna movement: you can find yogic elements in it but not so obviously.

When I came to India I became aware that there were multiple religions and religious streams, many traditions: Krishna too, but in other forms than contained in the Hare Krishna movement. There were many Tantrics too, and I slowly changed my thinking. I also started to develop my English language at that time.

Sadhus have a kind of improper English and therefore I picked up some bad grammatical habits including a few that were difficult to change in future times. If I'd spent time in the UK or USA my English would have been better than after being in India. I also improved my Hindi and Sanskrit. Sanskrit is not a spoken language but is important for spiritual practice.

I was seeking to learn more about Yoga but didn't have money, so couldn't study Yoga in commercial schools. Instead I met Sadhus from many traditions, and that helped to change my thinking and opinions about Yoga. For example, we sometimes travelled together and I asked, 'Have you any system for proper eating, like a special diet?' And they said a real yogi never cares about food. Simple life means careless in the sense of not caring about externals. Caring about food and such things is for those who desire a glamorous lifestyle, with their special diets. I was surprised.

I asked about sets of asanas, yogic postures, and they said, we haven't such sequences. They are only for commercial reasons. We have Guru-student (shishya) relationships, and a Guru can see what the student needs and then give those asanas that an individual needs. It was this kind of system. This challenged my ideas, including what I'd read in some books on Yoga. I realized there are no set sequences. There are no fixed sequences in ancient scriptures. It cannot be one system for everyone. They gave personal teachings to me, especially acceptable and appropriate for my constitution and level of development. I also saw some Sadhus who smoked. I said 'You are yogis; you should be very pure.' I said this is not good for a yogi. They said, 'No, no, it is not good for a yogi to care about the external shape, so the shape for a yogi is to not care about shape.' They didn't care about my views about a glamorous life or glamorous ideas about Yoga. It was completely controversial and deconstructing my old ideas.

This radical perspective felt correct, at least partially. It created a revolution in my mind. I digested it for a long time. I realized that Western culture has a false idea about Hinduism, Yoga and Tantra and have created a completely wrong understanding. Sometimes in Western society, Tantra is presented in a very sophisticated way. It is then a dry knowledge or a kind of erotic massage. It isn't worship of Indian deities, or supreme elements.

Visa Conundrums

In Australia I became interested in Interfaith. You cannot say India has an interfaith organization; India is an interfaith society. Even in Russia during my Yoga classes, I had already introduced elements of different religions and teachers: Christianity, Shinto, Kabbalah, magic and more. I was naturally inclined this way. Keith calls this universalism. That's okay. When I went to India I observed many different religious branches. It was normal to see Jesus sitting on a lotus surrounded by Durga and Ganesha. One does *Puja* for everyone.

I tried to extend my visa in India but they didn't allow it. They said, 'You only want to stay here, rather than in another country, you are not a genuine tourist.' Then I met a past student. She said, 'I am now in South Korea. I can arrange a student visa for you. They have a system similar to Yoga you could explore and maybe blend.'

I said, 'Oh yes, maybe I can combine them and stay half a year in South Korea and half in India.'

Because I stayed in touch with students by email or internet this opportunity arose. My student introduced me to a teacher in South Korea. He was very nice and gave me a black belt in his tradition and permission to teach anywhere. I studied and lived there for three and a half years.

I understood that a Russian passport is not good for travelling and began to research how to travel more easily and freely. My student suggested that I come to South Korea, become a student, and create an opportunity to obtain a six-month visa. This I successfully achieved. I was in India a few years before I went to South Korea.

Before that I had to keep leaving India in order to renew my visa, mostly six-month stays in India, then leave and re-apply: half a year in India, then back to Russia, Thailand, Nepal, and Singapore. On this occasion I was going to Thailand but my student said, why not let me arrange for you to come to South Korea. And I replied, 'Okay, let's do that.'

Guruji

At some point in time I met Guruji. He is my main teacher. He attracted me because of his purity of mind and nature. Sometimes people can have powers and knowledge, but their human nature is not so good. I think *Sadhana*: spiritual practices, first of all make human nature good. I felt Guruji's practice was very deep. Otherwise it would have been like black magic or dry knowledge.

I met him in North India. It was a spontaneous meeting. We discussed extensively. He explained many connections between Yoga, Tantra and other spiritual perspectives. I felt some power from him and much knowledge, but most importantly he was acutely alive. It was not like receiving school knowledge. He had wisdom, some enormous capacity of intuition, and could see into my heart and needs. At times questions arrived in my mind and he answered them without me asking. He didn't have other students then.

I asked him if he would be my teacher and he agreed, but that all happened naturally and smoothly, not premeditated. In a way I didn't really ask him. It was meant to be.

I felt some ancient yogic power. In that atmosphere events don't happen in ordinary ways. There are powers in those sacred geographical places, many generations of spiritual practitioners have left something behind. It creates an invisible atmosphere. I prayed to past great souls when I looked at their pictures and felt powers. I prayed that their blessings would bring me a desired-for Guru and when it happened it was all very natural, like a flowing river, because that energy brings boons. That energy brought me to him. It is like that.

I met Guruji a few years before I went to South Korea. As I said, I got my name Matsyendranath from a Sadhu, and Guruji laughed, and I asked, 'Why are you laughing?' He said, 'We pray to Matsyendranath in our tradition. So I am now blessed by his presence.' I said, 'Maybe I shall change my name then.' He responded, 'No it's okay. It isn't a problem. Maybe someone else will tremble when they hear your name, but that isn't a tragedy. You can keep this name.'

Keith thinks that it is an interesting name in the context of the story about the original Matsyendranath. "Because it's as if you are in the fish's belly really listening to Shiva and wanting to be his student."

Yes, that's correct. Maybe my fish was inertia and from there I listen. This is another dimension of Shiva. I actually had deep mystical experiences before India, and in India they were strengthened and validated. Even in childhood I had deep experience when I practiced Yoga. Within myself I experienced confirmation of my intuitions and feelings like an energy field surrounding me. Being with Guruji enhanced and progressed my experience and understanding. From Russia to India with a love of seeking truth then returning to Russia with my Guruji, wiser than when I'd left, and then studying in South Korea. It all seemed mystically connected, linking back to my youthful promptings and intuitions.

Youthful Developments

I was about sixteen when I realized I had some natural capacity to teach, maybe not in the academic sense but in a more unusual, yet natural way. By then I had gathered some experience in martial arts and Qigong. I didn't know anything about reincarnation or many spiritual topics, but I did feel something when for instance I was surrounded by nature. It felt as if nature and I were identical and equally significant. Everything felt the same as me: mountains, rivers, sky, grass, all of nature, and I felt tiny, physically. Then all movement stopped and actions and meditation happened spontaneously. I forgot about my body. It was as if I was aware of my body only in the sense that everything was my body. I didn't have a spiritual teacher at that time. My martial art teacher wasn't interested in spiritual matters.

One time when I was about eighteen, my mother saw a newspaper advertisement promoting a Shaolin teacher in Bryansk. Many people called themselves such things but they were not authentic. My mother said, 'Don't be too skeptical, I feel sure this will be good for you.' I thought 'Mum, you don't know. I have studied many things. There are many charlatans who give themselves exotic names', but my mother was insistent. She really felt this would be interesting for me. I said, 'Okay I should go.' So I went to this event.

This was the moment I turned deeply towards Yoga, because before that I did Yoga only as exercises. It was as if Yoga up to that moment had been in preparation for something greater. It had been overly associated with martial arts in my thinking, but this was mistaken. Therefore I came to this guy who was maybe in his forties. This in itself was a little uncommon in Russia, because most who practiced Yoga and martial arts were much younger, and generally related to ideas that it would help them with their futures.

On arrival I looked at his face and especially his eyes, which were sublimely peaceful. His master was from Vietnam and had studied with a Chinese Shaolin master who had immigrated to Vietnam. He'd learnt many inner practices and was most impressive. I watched a video of him. He'd come to Minsk in Belarus to lead seminars.

He placed four thick stone slabs, much bigger than bricks, one atop the other on his knees. He was sitting with these bricks on his knees and he did a special hand movement, a karate chop. The top three slabs split in half and the bottom slab pulverized into dust. He was a strong man but not like Schwarzenegger, so this was impossible by ordinary physical means. I thereafter understood that there were practices that increase energy and power in the body.

I met his student, the visiting Shaolin teacher in Bryansk, and began to practice with him as he kept watch over my progress. He accepted me as his student and told me he would show me some practices. He asked me to do a martial art kick against him, so I did this very quickly whilst he was still talking. He kept talking even as he blocked my kick. I don't know the word for this in English. You know, it is when the one who is being attacked uses the attacking movement to gain control. Then he just returned to a meditative posture with very calm eyes and said, 'Never do it like that.'

It happened in a big hall full of gymnasts and others, and suddenly everyone stopped whatever they were doing and a deep silence took over. You see, when he did that blocking movement he let out a sound, like a spontaneous karate sound, and everyone was stunned and silenced by the power of it.

Before the silence there was a collective gasp and then he said with intense but calm intent, 'Never do it like that, for it is not effective.' I was very impressed. He added that my movements would be ineffective in real situations, for instance, against street gangsters in Russia. I did a few other movements against him but he blocked them all. I was impressed by his inner power.

After a few sessions with him, he gave his home address to another student but not to me. I met this student on the street and said, 'You know his address, we could go there and pay him a visit.' So we came to his apartment and his front door was unlocked. This was unusual in Russia, to not be in fear to the degree of leaving one's door unlocked. I opened his door. There was church music playing, again unusual and surprising, because such people in Russia usually have antipathy against the church, so I thought, 'Maybe he is a bit crazy.'

He said, 'Yes, come in. Sit. I will make tea.' We talked and he gave us some inner practices. I asked him about spiritual powers. I told him I'd read about yogis and he said, 'In that case you should practice Yoga.' He explained about chakras and that by way of Yoga I could get good results. He instructed me in Qigong, and for Yoga he gave me some books. I was really interested and began to earnestly practice. I also tried to do pranayama, breath meditation.

I read in one book a particular technique by an Indian writer. He wrote that if you do this technique eight hours a day for six months an awakening of Kundalini would occur. I thought eight hours a day is so much.

I asked a few people about this but when I went to Ukraine to attend a Yoga seminar with my teacher, some practitioners said such practices were unnecessary. I said, 'How can you say unnecessary when ancient texts suggest it?' People read these texts but do not do what is suggested and then say 'unnecessary'. No one actually practiced. I thought, 'I should do an experiment,' and I did for about eight months.

I did pranayama, or breath-focused meditation, eight hours a day, usually in four two-hour sessions approximately, sometimes a little less, but more or less eight hours every day. There were already people attracted to my activities by then.

Throughout this time I almost stopped all other activities. A few students brought me food, as if I was a yogi in a cave. It was difficult to teach Yoga at that time, but some who sat close to me felt something. Occasionally someone would even lose consciousness, because the energy was potent. A number of electronic devices would malfunction and light bulbs would shatter. The word got about and one reporter from a newspaper visited, but I wouldn't answer her questions about this 'spiritual phenomena.' Then after the interview ended the reporter realized that her recording device hadn't picked anything up. She suggested that there must be something wrong with her device. Of course skeptics will always seek a logical explanation.

I also realized that I now had healing capacities. For example Tatiana, my sister, had a disease and I hugged her, breathed a few times through her with consciously directed energy and her disease disappeared. People's headaches would dissolve. This all happened easily and naturally. I experimented privately too and what you call psychokenisis occurred. I could move some physical objects with mental intention. The boldness and audacity of youth!

Seeking Confirmation

I don't consider spiritual and psychic powers either good or bad, but these youthful experiences engendered increased faith. I understood that such powers exist. It was a confirmation that I was on the right track. There were experiences of expanded consciousness that were undeniable. They were lights that were strong enough to inspire me to keep going in this direction. Those lights were actually tangible, like crown chakra experiences that naturally appear, have a strong presence and are intensely peaceful. They embraced my whole being and it felt as if the universe was close to me.

I could not speak from there. It rendered me silent. I could try to describe it in various ways but at that time I couldn't. You know, if you see beauty that is indescribable you understand it is everywhere, in every movement, totally alive and for all these reasons one should be peaceful and not necessarily do anything, but just relax and wait. Allow life to continue and these experiences will be a gift for good, solid future directions. This I understood clearly and simply.

Then I came to India and different people tried to describe their sacred texts: this should be like this and that like that. In this way for instance *prakasha*, subtle lights, should be experienced here at a particular place on the body.

One pandit tried to teach me, but I just looked at him with a skeptical expression, because I understood what he was saying from inner experience, and he had only conceptual knowledge, so I looked in a certain way and he asked, 'Are you fine?' I replied, 'Oh yes, more than fine.'

With a few years of experiences behind me I was receiving confirmation from scripture, and understood that many people hadn't the experience, only belief in scripture. It was as if people in India and Russia were more inclined to just believe in teachings without testing them. I thought there must be a teacher who really knows from experience, but at first in India I didn't find such a teacher.

In my perception the entire universe was my Guru. I was maybe looking for a universal Guru. In that time there was not so much information available. There was no information about Kundalini and what there was in books is not the same as receiving from authentic teachers. The internet was not available for most ordinary people. I was seeking confirmation, to know that my path was authentic.

Before India, I had locked myself in my apartment and wouldn't open the door. Many people came and knocked but I wouldn't open. I decided to be a recluse and then even more people came. And then when I finally emerged and began Yoga classes again I was very slim, not anorexic, but streamlined, because I didn't want to eat, anyway minimally, not like here in Australia. I didn't oversleep either and some students said my eyes were really shining. When I taught others in my classes, meditation or other practices, my energy penetrated everyone and some had unusual experiences.

So even before India I had many positive and sublime experiences. A journalist even published an article about me in a Bryansk newspaper. I think that was in 1994.

Some of my students were unhappy when I went to India. Before that I'd gone to Cyprus, then came back and was in Moscow for some months and then suddenly I was going to India with a one-way ticket.

To some it seemed like I was saying goodbye forever. There was no internet at that time. It was felt that in going to India no one would find me. I didn't even tell my students how I was departing. I didn't want to disclose such information. After one year I returned briefly to Bryansk and spoke about my experiences in India.

India and South Korea

Probably the most powerful experiences I had before leaving Russia were related to Tantra, but this was without much confirmation. In India this type of experience was reinforced but not so much from people. In India I felt a Being, not all the time, but it was often undeniable. Not everyone felt this because some people are aware and others not so, but for me, I felt another dimension of being, an external Being that oversaw and corrected my life, and helped me receive proper knowledge. I think it was connected to some deeper karmic bond I had with India and was identified with Shiva. He arranged my first visit to India and saved me from commercial Yoga centers. That is how it felt.

I directly communicated with Sadhus. They are pilgrims and Sannyasins. They were more honest than commercially-focused Gurus. They were not interested in creating a glamorous type of Yoga. I thought, 'I don't have money to go to Yoga centers or be taught by professional teachers like Iyengar. Many people have money and can do that but I am poor. I should just stay in temples.'

I felt it was in my nature that my way was right, because in the past I'd intuited that this situation would happen and suddenly I remembered what I'd felt. I thought, 'Okay I should surrender, accept this situation and see what happens.'

Sometimes profoundly intense people were attracted to me. This happened naturally in different places. I visited a few Gurus like Sai Baba, but they existed within different environments and with different types of people to those who I was seeking. Some of these people were good but many I found to be artificial. In India there were many beautiful places, not less beautiful than such popular spiritual environments. It was possible to come across a special and unusual person in a place where you didn't expect it.

In the commercial Yoga centers, by contrast, one finds mostly business people. There are many corrupted Gurus and I encountered the spectrum from artificial to authentic. Of course there are many dimensions occurring side by side in India. The British and Americans were more powerful than the Indians who often try to imitate them. They try to imitate empires that are viewed as politically stronger.

On the other side of India you can find traditional life and this was difficult to understand for a foreigner like myself. Nowadays when there is understanding it is still difficult to truly value their traditions, and therefore it is important to see who they really are.

Some people have magical powers but they don't have good human natures. Others have good natures and have understanding of spiritual and mystical matters. When I first came to India I thought all yogis and spiritual people were authentic, but I soon discovered it was not so. Nonetheless, India was a part of my soul.

South Korea was another phase of my life. It was there that I met a teacher who had a very spiritual nature. Sometimes he described his tradition to me, and I immediately understood that this was the same as one can find in traditional Yoga texts. Of course if you observe modern Yoga you can find a lot of difference, but he knew much about light, macrocosm, microcosm and union, plus he was clear and genuine.

He was a university professor who taught his tradition under the umbrella of the physical education department. In specialising in his own tradition he was wiser than his university position might have appeared. There was an extra-sensory capacity present. It was simply obvious for those who spent time and talked with him. Sometimes I asked him challenging questions. He said, 'You don't need answers, just practice.'

By this time I knew Eastern culture, but he understood another type of Eastern tradition, different from India. I learnt how their culture was related to their spirituality and practices. There were charlatans in South Korea too but he was a well-respected person there. In India someone like this would be perceived almost like Shiva, and expected to demonstrate many unusual things that were difficult for others to do.

His teacher had extraordinary powers and could do unusual things. For example he once stayed submerged under water for fourteen minutes. Those present began to panic, wondering if had drowned. So they pulled him out and he said, 'Why did you pull me out?' Once he sat surrounded by fire without any harm to his body. Or he could pick up heavy things with his teeth. There are even some films of this on the internet. This university professor, who became my kind and wise mentor, was his student. His master went to the mountains and disappeared after many years of teaching and his student became my teacher. His name is Kim Ki Young. His teaching explained much about meditation.

Having a Russian passport made it difficult to obtain a visa to another country. For example, once I applied for a visa to Canada and they would not talk to me. Eventually they sent my passport back with a note which said, 'In your country there are nuclear weapons, so we cannot grant you a visa.' They said this to someone who practiced Yoga and promoted peace. I was refused visas a number of times. From that time of being refused entry to Canada I became interested in why this situation existed, and began to study international politics more deeply. I explored this topic with an interest I'd never had before.

I first visited Australia in 2008 when I got a tourist visa, and saw it as a sign. In Korea they had given me a one-year student visa, so I applied from there for an Australian tourist visa.

When arriving in Australia a friend said, 'My Guru is here in Australia so if you are interested a meeting can be arranged. This was a meeting with the leader of a Shaivism ashram in Melbourne. The people of this ashram welcomed me with flowers and a traditional reception. I did a fire sacrifice ceremony and explained the meaning. We had good conversations and then they said they had an interesting person you should meet and that was John Dupuche. I said, 'I saw his book' and one of my Indian friends told me he was a Catholic priest who studied Sanskrit and Tantra. This was interesting because he was a Catholic priest with such broad interests. They arranged a meeting with him and together we attended an Interfaith conference.

There followed more constructive meetings in Melbourne. I met many interesting people and this first visit to Melbourne lasted a few months and made a positive impression. After leaving I thought maybe I could try and stay here. I could explore how it might be possible to stay, to immigrate to Australia. Everything seemed to be going smoothly, but it took seven years to finally succeed. Seven years since my first visit to Australia.

I returned to South Korea and finished my formal university studies. After three and a half years of study I graduated with a degree in Physical Education and seriously began thinking of immigrating to Australia.

I had developed a good relationship with my university professor and he said, 'No problem, you can stay half a year in India and half a year in South Korea in the meantime. You can be a part of this university because your topic of interest is related to your degree. It is a continuation of your study. You can do research here about our traditional ways and find useful connections between Yoga and our traditions.'

Therefore these streams were allowed to meet and I could also spend time in India. This was all fortunate and studying in South Korea became a way into more stability. My teacher in Korea was also very interested in Yoga so we developed creative ways to exchange information.

Once the director of the university visited India with me and was somewhat shocked. We travelled around to places like Varanasi. He couldn't understand why there were such train delays, sometimes three hours late, because in South Korea everything runs very smoothly. He was shocked to see cows on the streets and couldn't understand why they were treated as holy animals, and of course there was the dire poverty of India. He was a little naive, but after this trip his feelings about India changed.

Maybe he'd heard something about India before but it's different when you actually go there. On returning, when his students asked about India he would say, 'First you go there and then I will share my impressions.'

Becoming a Yogi in India

When I first visited India I experienced a cultural shock. I wasn't really aware of what was happening because everything was different from Russia. It was like a fairy tale. I'd never before stumbled into such a culture as India. I had heard many beautiful and interesting stories but what I experienced didn't relate to them. It was totally different. There were some Russians and other foreigners on the plane who were also going to India. Many had money but I felt they had a more carefree attitude than me because I didn't have money, and thought 'How will I survive?' I was aware there would be challenges ahead but I tried to pacify my mind. 'Don't worry. Be peaceful. Do everything properly. You should survive and overcome all challenges.' I was mindfully careful about what I encountered in India.

At this point I was still named Maxim. My name changed after a brief time with a Sadhu. After meeting him, we talked about Yoga, Tantra and many other spiritual topics. I told him that in the years of the Soviet Union I'd seen a book, Gorakhvijaya, The Victory of Gorakhnath, which was about the story of Gorakhnath. It had been translated in the time of the Soviet Union, but as a type of mythological text, not a mystical or spiritual book. I said to the Sadhu I'd heard about Matsyendranath and he said, 'Oh, you know about this'.

The text was not available in English but someone had translated it into Russian, the story of Gorakhnath and Matsyendranath. He was pleased that I knew this story and said, 'You and Matsyendranath are alike.' I told him I liked this name and he said, 'You can keep this name.' Maybe he was joking or partly joking, but I considered him as being serious and worthy of respect. We didn't only talk about this topic, and he impressed me with his knowledge and deep capacity to understand, so I thought, 'Okay, if he allows me to have this name I can accept it.' To begin with I used the name Matsyendranath. Yogi came later. I came across other Tantrics who initiated me, and they said, 'Okay, this name Matsyendranath or Matsyendrananda can be used by you.'

When I met my Guruji he laughed and told me they worshipped Matsyendranath. It was a joke, as if they had been praying to me but it was all positive and well intentioned. Guruji said. 'Okay, you can keep this name.' Some Sadhus told me that it wasn't a good idea and didn't like it, but others said it was fine and no problem. Actually there was a mystical connection I felt to this name. Matsyendra was the ruler of fish and I am Piscean and also naturally like Tantra. Matsyendranath was a deep practicing Tantric. Gorakhnath, his student, was a bit different. He accepted the essence of that knowledge and combined it with aesthetic practices. He found a kind of intermediate combination. Therefore it became the metaphysical source of Hatha Yoga. It became the way of the union of opposites: sun, moon, Shiva, Shakti, male, female, and so on. It became like a middle way. Gorakhnath created a flexible way acceptable for any spiritual seeker.

Some think Yoga is beyond religion but actually there is no conflict between them. Yoga is very tolerant. If any religious practice can provide transformation then it is good. It is not mere formality, in which case religion may be useless. So Nath followers are religious but they say, 'We are beyond everything. We are beyond conceptions and have a free mind.'

When I visited Gorakhpur and became initiated by my Guru he gave me the sacred thread, something like Brahmanical but a little different. At that moment, he said, 'Now you have become a part of our tradition. You are now a yogi.' I was very happy. I felt immediately as if that place talked to me. It was only a little later that Guruji explained that many had experienced samadhi (deep meditation) in this place. It was where past yogis over many centuries were buried. Even though there had been many external changes, there was a presence developed over many centuries. I didn't understand why there was such a strong energy. I'd felt something similar in Egypt by the pyramids. I couldn't explain but in those environments knowledge immediately came to me.

I stayed in Gorakhpur and did practices, communicated with Sadhus, often visiting each other, and all this adjacent to the burial place of past yogis. This yogic practice had been happening for more than a thousand years. Many past yogis had been interred there in a sitting position, in samadhi. The energy field was palpable.

Baba

On this first occasion I didn't expect to be in the Gorakhnath temple for a long time. The temple administration tried to redirect me back to other places, which are more popular among tourists, not realizing my true intention for being there. But I wanted to be there so they said, 'Okay, you can come in the early morning,' expecting that would stop me. I came at four in the morning to attend morning worship and later at nine I attended a Yoga class for local people, under the guidance of a local Yogacharya. They saw how I did asanas and suggested that I obtain darshan from the head of the temple. They called him Baba. His name was Yogi Avedyanath and he was a very old patriarch. He passed away a couple of years ago in his nineties, but when I first met him he was in good health. He was also involved in politics and environmentalism. There was a lot of security around him and when they brought me to his meeting room, I realized this was a serious set up. It was all unexpected for me. He was very humble and offered me tea and food. He asked his followers, "Where did you find him?" They answered that they found me in the Yoga class where I was doing very good yoga. He asked me a lot of questions. I told him I was interested in Yoga and about Gorakhnath and Matsyendranath. He described things briefly but profoundly. He said, "If you are interested you can visit, maybe tomorrow after the Yoga class, we can meet again."

When I visited the following morning he was happy. He talked a lot to me, at the same time people brought documents for him to sign. People approached him and asked questions, and he would answer briefly, but would continue to talk to me without losing the thread. At that time he seemed to me like Julius Caesar. He said, 'You can stay in our temple. We can prepare a room for you.'

I was glad to receive this offer and brought my luggage. After that I met my Guru. It was all unpredictable. Baba Avedyanath and my Guruji had a good relationship. Guruji had another temple but was staying at Gorakhpur. There are actually four cities named Gorakhpur, in four different states, and these are strong centers of devotion towards Gorakhnath and Matsyendranath. The Naths believe that Gorakhnath is immortal so he can appear at different times. So for instance there are stories about him meeting Guru Nanak, and so on.

Keith jokingly suggests that maybe some people may think he has come back as me. I laughed and said, 'Maybe.'

1977: Yogi is one year old

With my grandfather and sister, Tatiana

In Caucasus

With my mother and sister

In India (above)   At the pyramid of Menkaure, Egypt (below)

In Varanasi

Being interviewed on ABC Radio 2015

Satsang in France 2013

Teaching (above) and performing ritual (below, right)

Odessa 2017

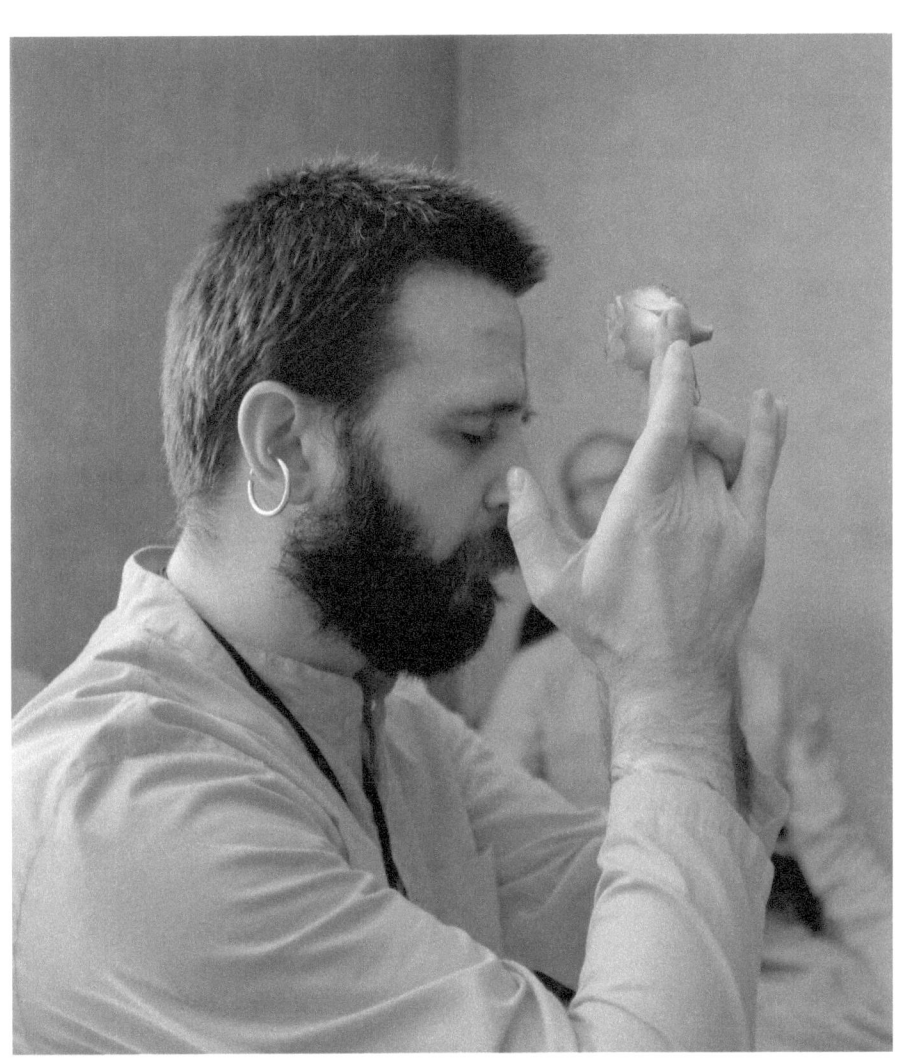

PART 3

YOGA

Yoga is not just a few techniques. It is a way of life and then your lifestyle becomes Yoga.

Yoga and Lifestyle

You know, in this tradition initiations are related to how aligned one's lifestyle is to Yoga. Some lifestyles are harmonious with yogic precepts, and some less so. There are deviations from yogic purity that are obstacles to overcome. For example, nowadays yoga asanas are 'decorated' superficially, and this is not in harmony with being an authentic yogi. Therefore there is a Yoga lifestyle.

When I was initiated as a yogi I felt peaceful and forgot everything that went before. It was like I'd stepped into a more real version of myself. There was a shift in attitude and feeling. If some difficulty occurred, it didn't feel like such a big drama. My intuitions were guiding more than ever. Even if I didn't understand what was happening around me, such as why they did certain rituals, I felt an energy and spiritual condition, and it was as if the spiritual atmosphere taught me.

If my Guruji gave small corrections I experienced a change immediately. He would give an instruction and it was perfect, it would work. It was as if I remembered something that was already there, inherently, and now it was conscious.

Some people are very powerful and have divine presence but are not necessarily Gurus. A Guru will not just give you something but will awaken what you already have, by his realization. He shares his realization. Realization in Tantra, for instance if you meditate on a particular deity, leads to an experience, a downflow of Grace.

When this happens one feels as if this presence is in you. One could describe it as descent of Grace or an awakening, or both at the same time. It is beyond any conceptual limitations or limited human nature. It is real nature. One could say it can be transmitted by a person, but actually it is something through a person. Or you could say it is the ground of that person. This is a transmission developed over many centuries. It is with the blessing of Shiva and a pure transmission of Shiva's power. You can be within a formal tradition but realize too, or feel it anyway without tradition. If you understand deeply you can feel the presence of Shiva.

When I gradually, over time, experienced such reality, I felt the oneness of everything. So this tradition is beautiful but the experience is beyond the tradition. It is not confined by tradition. It is a transcendental experience. Then some of my past students came too, and became so inspired that they asked if they could help me somehow. When I wanted to extend my visa some of my students said, 'We can help you.' There were opportunities to teach in Russia but at that time I was more interested in furthering my own explorations.

"How did Indians respond to a non-Indian yogi teaching Indians?"

That is a complicated topic because India is a different type of society. In India they have multiple cultures. Even the Brahmanical tradition has many cultural and sectarian expressions, and there is the caste system too. All these branches have their own rules. I was from another culture. Maybe there are similarities but also some incomparable differences.

But yogis are beyond such limited systems. It was therefore easier than, for instance, if I'd followed a Vedic tradition. India is the mother of Yoga. In the highest level of Yoga and deepest awareness of it, you can say that Yoga is beyond any nationality. If we want to use traditional knowledge in any culture before understanding traditional ways, we block the proper use of such knowledge. But if we first understand the traditional ways of a culture, we can use such knowledge in good ways. Otherwise if I am unaware, I could fabricate, and become something like a New Age imitator.

"So the basis of understanding is experiential?"

It depends on how honest one is in relation to the tradition, and how honest you are with yourself. Some can be honest in India with Indians but cheat others.

"You can be honest and dishonest simultaneously?"

So you should be honest with yourself. You should recognize what is pure: pure but mixed, so some Indians take something pure but use it impurely.

"Highest Yoga then requires a high degree of honest self-examination."

Right! You should listen to yourself. Everything in tradition must be beautiful. Traditional ways of Yoga in India should be distinguished from the commercial Yoga schools. There are two different dimensions at play: one traditional and the other westernized. True Sadhana, spiritual yogic practices, and commercial so-called yoga exercises are completely different.

Yoga as Paradox

What I can say about Yoga, if I can say anything, is that this topic is linguistically paradoxical. From one point of view Yoga should be distinguished from ordinary mechanical viewpoints that tend towards spiritual consumerism. At the same time an independent state of mind should be related to egolessness. How can you be independent from everyone but without ego? For many this is quite paradoxical.

"What is meant by ego in this context?"

Ego can be understood as an instrument of supreme consciousness. When we use the ego like an instrument for our supreme self, skillfully use it, then there is a unifying mirror, but if we only become identified with the instrument, then we become only the instrument. You cannot be in this world without ego. It is like a knife: you can cut vegetables for cooking, but you can also kill someone. Or like fire: it isn't good or bad. It is the same with ego. When ego deviates it isn't aligning with the supreme self. It is a manifestation of the instrument falsely identifying itself as the supreme. You could say it is the great illusion.

In Sanskrit 'Maya', from the root 'Ma', means, 'to measure'. So illusion is confusing what is measurable with the limitless. If that act of measuring creates limitations, then it is illusion, but if there are no limitations then it is in harmony with the limitless. For instance: money is not evil, nor good, money is just money.

"If I understand this correctly Yogi, there is a power that is keeping me alive. Indeed this power is my life. This power as consciousness is not the contents of consciousness. How I use this consciousness through my mind and body is a secondary dimension. If this secondary dimension is aligned and in harmony with supreme Consciousness – something that can appear paradoxical in language – then everything flows because you are one with the Cosmos. But if the ego begins to deviate, and believes it is in control, and doesn't believe in Supreme consciousness, then this becomes a deviation."

It is again the game of this measuring faculty. We then cannot see the whole picture because we have become limited.

"A bit like Alice in Wonderland who then enters into strange dream like fantasy landscapes; I can become lost in an illusory world. It can become a problem if I believe it is reality."

Yes, rabbit holes. That rabbit can go down a hole but he might die in there, so if he realizes this he should withdraw, go out. Ego is like a prison. Egotistic people are immovable or movable in very narrow spaces, and find themselves in dangerous circumstances.

A Worldly Yogi

I hadn't lived in Russia for fifteen years when I came to Australia for the second time in 2010, but the idea to try and live here had occurred to me when I returned to South Korea two years earlier. South Korea is a beautiful country, with interesting people and a strong culture, but as a foreigner I would never be accepted by their society. It is not a multicultural country like Australia. Yes, I could have obtained residency in Korea but socially I would have always been like an outcast. Australia represented a society that was open to all traditions. I think it is the most multicultural country I've been to. Also I think Australia has a promising future, a good potential.

I already understood that a Russian passport was a liability and so in 2010 my intention to stay here became stronger. Now I have my permanent residency it is like a prize for enduring five years of torture. No more embassies and no more being perceived like some kind of monster or dangerous alien, or that I ought to feel ashamed of being Russian. No more of that horrible stigma.

In a way it was beneficial to have had the experiences with the Canadian and American embassies, and I can understand this thinking, but more importantly it inspired me to try and understand everything about life on the political, cultural and human scale. I thought, 'A yogi should be aware of everything,' because yogis are not ancient anymore.

We are living now in the twenty-first century. It's neither a yogi living on a mountaintop in a cave with little or no contact with the world, nor being a professional yogi in a commercial Yoga center.

Some people, especially in the West think of chakras as pretty colored discs on a plastic strip that you can attach to a refrigerator like a magnetic decoration, maybe with a few words attached. It is like that for many people who attend Yoga centers. Some Eastern decorations are glamorous but most people are unaware of the deep complexity of the chakras. It is important to not only study chakras but also Indian culture. If people study Qigong they should study Chinese culture too, and beyond that, all human knowledge everywhere.

A sincere seeker should be intelligent. Some people imitate yogis but if you are sincere you should study the environment where the practices have their homes.

Much had begun to change for me when I came to India and met Sadhus. They changed my opinions about what Yoga is. I'd been influenced to a degree by the Western environment where business elements are involved, but is still called Yoga. I had some pure experience of Yoga but my understanding changed. Letting go of the false leaves the real. How can I now teach those who come to me as a Western yogi? In my new capacity, it must be spontaneous. I don't know how to teach others. I don't think, 'I am doing this'. I don't have a strict formula. That pure space directs me. When I am empty something happens. This is more effective than planning and plotting. Often a simple approach is best.

Real and Fake Teachers

Some Gurus and spiritual guides have tried to cheat rather than teach. Cheating isn't only about money; it is also about power and influence and can include types of black magic. For example the wrong uses of Tantra, because Tantric practices can be powerful. Some spiritual seekers may feel strong energy from a teacher and think he is enlightened, because he has developed a particular power, but one must be cautious.

An authentic Guru will be honest from the beginning. He will never give fake compliments. Some give compliments even if the seekers are going in the wrong direction, especially if money is involved. A real teacher is not a hypocrite. He will be sincere and not falsely groom you. If he is concerned with your money, then anything he says may not be true. It is possible to create a beautiful environment but be a cheat. So this is something to be aware of.

Another trap can be when communicating with a Guru and he evokes a big experience in you, but then it quickly fades and is finished as if nothing had happened. Sometimes a glamorous Guru can be alluring and attract the unwary seeker. The seeker gets a 'high' but then nothing. True spiritual life involves becoming increasingly aware over a long duration. After one year you realize you have become wiser including during communications with your Guru. Real change will be happening: not just superficial impressions.

When seekers have sudden highs but otherwise are complaining about their lives, and essentially unchanging, then something is not right. Spiritual attainment is not an occasional exulted condition that can be like a crazy outburst, followed by bad consequences. True attainment is continuous, it never stops.

Therefore a true Guru will give you a proper way to grow and be consistent and stable. Everything a Guru gives he can give deeply, even the simplest things. Some Gurus can teach about very simple things but with a double meaning. There is more than meets the ordinary eye.

The receiver can have a mystical experience from any type of activity performed by the Guru. For example he can talk about food but behind the words something else is being revealed or demonstrated. The true Guru has already identified with spiritual energies and therefore those energies emanate from him.

Therefore even within an ordinary meeting with my Guruji his light touch could elicit an experience, maybe some energy flowing up my spine. In his presence my mind would become clear and meditative. Even when he was silent and I would sit close to him everything happened, some purification happened.

But to find a Satguru, an authentic wise teacher is quite difficult. We always attract in our lives that which relates to our spiritual condition. So with a good understanding you can find the right teachers. Some people practice Yoga and meditate but lack correct understanding. They may have false conceptions, including about Gurus. Therefore finding a good teacher doesn't usually happen immediately. Everyone can stumble at first and be attracted to cheats and fakes.

It can be helpful to study the relationships between teachers and students in sacred books: what happens, how it must be, and try and be aware of why they talk as they do. After that try and become aware of the meanings of the scriptures.

It should be noted that even if someone finds an unenlightened person who sets you in the right direction it is good. For instance, he might say, 'If you can find a Guru who can impart some knowledge that would be good,' or maybe he can reveal knowledge of asanas, pranayama or some general rituals. But if such a Guru cannot bring you to a knowledge of the supreme then it is of limited significance. The point is that when the seeker becomes stronger he will find a stronger Guru.

Then one should be grateful for all the other teachers who have helped you along the way. You should see how they have helped to cause you to be where you are and feel gratitude, because via those you came to this. In this way one can continue to discover someone even stronger. Also always be aware of your situations. If you are a cheat you will attract cheats. If you have low motivations you will attract others like that.

Karma

Some people are born in poor countries but they surrender and accept their situation and think, 'It's okay. It's not so bad.' If the environment is corrupt and violent, maybe disgusting, some think, 'It's no problem. I will try to change this.' Others are born into beautiful environments with plenty of everything. They may be very rich with no great external difficulties to contend with, but they become lazy and never develop themselves.

To change karma, different environments offer varied opportunities and influences. For example Buddha was born in palatial circumstances. His family was wealthy and powerful but at a certain time in his development he wanted to study spiritual topics. He wasn't satisfied.

People can be unsatisfied in all types of environments, including the best. Some people try to find something in any circumstances but some never try to find anything, regardless.

I, like you, am responsible for what I attract.

From the time of the Vedas the concept of karma developed more and more. The essential meaning of karma is action that creates future. So in my tradition there are many types of karma, different angles and contexts. For instance some karma has been created already and this should be realized. We can also prevent bad karma in the future.

When past karmic influences become difficult in present circumstances, we should understand and accept them. The effects will pass in time, but karma always has effects, such as illness. In this way we can purify our karma like cleaning a polluted river. We should therefore be peaceful if difficulties emerge. We can then become stronger and overcome the causes that are within our souls.

I saw one situation in India that explained karma to me in a good way and how you can overcome it. There were small boys playing close to the street. Some Sadhus were passing and the boys threw stones at them. The Sadhus kept walking without reaction. This made the boys keener to throw stones. Then some adults came by and did the same to the boys as they had done to the Sadhus, and went on their way. So no one can avoid karma. If people do bad things it is sometimes necessary to protect yourself. If it's serious, protection is good, but if it's not then allow karma to unfold by another hand.

Culture

Australia is a young country, compared to Russia, Europe and India. I mean those who came here, the first settlers, came not so long ago. Of course it is tragic what happened to the Aboriginal people. Different foreigners came here, like the British, Greeks and so on, who arrived recently, unlike Europe, Russia and China.

Young countries are open for new opportunities, similar to young people who are open to many things. This is a good situation. There are not many countries where you can find Indian temples, Buddhist temples, mosques, synagogues and churches tolerantly co-existing, but Australia could develop more deeply, exploring culture with more depth, not artificially. Sometimes when you have plenty there are shallow feelings. To not have enough isn't good either, like North Korea. There are opportunities for depth but opportunities can also be wasted.

Australia could become stronger, even a leading country in the world, culturally and spiritually. In Australia you have much variety, many glamorous things, but sometimes if you look at another culture, an Eastern culture, you can find very different things, that can be difficult to understand or accept from a Western perspective. It can be challenging to understand and accept something foreign to one's culture but I think it is possible for us to understand properly and without disturbance. It is possible to understand that another culture that is different to our own must also be respected, even if this is challenging and difficult.

If you cannot respect something you will never understand it. If something from a Western perspective doesn't look beautiful you should respect it without emotional reactions and with a neutral mind.

The Supreme is always omnipresent and in that sense I am a Universalist. I am omnipresent in the midst of good and bad. It is not easy to see this presence everywhere and maybe this is another aspect of the supreme, possibly controversial from a mundane point of view.

If I am a vegetarian I do not bully people who are not. For example. I can explain what I think about my lifestyle and what I believe is good in it.

Another example: you know the adoration given to Gurus is not acceptable in the West for many because we do not research why people do that. If you study with a type of scientific exactitude, then maybe the perspective can change, and such adoring behavior doesn't seem so crazy. Of course we should avoid criminal people but without an open mind how will you know? So we should be tolerant but not stupid, not with blinkers or rose-colored glasses.

Interfaith Tantra Interview

Rachel Kohn interviewed me a few days ago. She has a radio program, 'The Spirit of Things' on ABC Radio National. I was there with three others being interviewed about an upcoming Tantric conference. She asked similar questions to my present biographer.

Of course the topic was Tantra. Rachel asked about how my tradition is connected to Tantra, what my name means and how I deal with questions from people who come to my Ashram. Also how modern understanding of Tantra compares with classical and traditional Tantra? She is a smart interviewer and I think, prepares well. I view a part of my role to clarify what Tantra is and isn't.

In India there are so many Gurus. My Guru wasn't like many others: those who deviate from traditional ways usually in the effort to make money. He was well respected in India even before he became known in other countries. He passed on to me traditional approaches to Tantra. I am faithful in spreading his way.

Ordinary Indians recognized him as an authentic traditional teacher of Tantra. It was a natural capacity for them to know this. Such religious ways are normal for them. If my Guru gave some suggestions and advice to people it was a totally normal situation for them.

One cannot generalize along certain lines about who is an authentic Tantric teacher or not. For instance, some go to America and teach quite properly and others stay in India but do not.

Now there are many religious branches of so-called Tantra: Buddhist, Taoist, Christian, Islamic, Jewish and Hindu.

Freedom and Discipline

There are common elements across the spectrum of religious Tantra, like archetypes. A common element is associated with Puja. One way of defining Puja is 'ceremony of adoration,' and an association is purification. This can be devotion towards deities and sometimes includes contemplation. When you identify with your normal reality and also something Supreme, then a type of purification is one effect of that. So Puja is one element of Tantra.

By purification is meant all parts of oneself, purification of mind and body and pranayama is an important practice in this process; also Nyasa where you touch different parts of your body so as to make them sacred. The real purpose of Tantra is for the transformation of mundane consciousness and to divinize it.

"Alchemy, with its symbolism of transmuting base metals into gold is also about the transformation of energy."

Yes, one can say 'gold' is the symbol for a shift in consciousness for the better. Someone changes energy and mind and therefore one's nature. The true Alchemist or Tantric transforms mundane consciousness into divine consciousness. For this approach one needs to be flexible. Consciousness awakens, as it must in order to see the divine. Not all activities and manifestations have flexible consciousness.

This brings us to the topics of discipline and freedom. First we should understand something about what freedom is. Then we can understand what discipline is. Many people have a misleading idea of freedom. For instance freedom for some is like anarchy. It should be clear that freedom could lead to suffering. We need freedom that results in peacefulness, related to purity.

As for discipline it is possible to get directly what you want. For instance, by way of discipline one may avoid passing through many incarnations. Another example: if you want to jump from point A to point B, like two separated rocks, you cannot carry too much luggage. You should leave the luggage behind. It is the same principle with greater aims; one can obtain more happiness than ordinarily possible.

So discipline can be a way of avoiding difficult consequences, but this is the direct way. There is discipline in every activity, and also freedom. It is like with money: you can spend it or save it. There is a balance possible. And there is wisdom necessary otherwise you may lose all your money. So both discipline and freedom can become too lop-sided. Some people make discipline overly *rajasic*: too passionate and obsessional. This too can be out of control. Discipline should therefore be balanced with freedom, like two wings of a bird that can fly beautifully and naturally.

According to Tantra and Yoga, some traditional ritualistic activities and yogic practices reflect a process that occurs in nature and in the universe. There is creativity and dissolution and with that type of discipline you are aligning with nature. I have some specific cyclic rituals and practices that reflect nature's movements: how one should go to sleep and waken, how you should connect to nature with meditation and how natural things always enhance and are related to harmony.

What is natural cannot be destructive. Ritual is not like in the Russian army that by association can create fear of the word discipline. If you understand discipline correctly then you develop respect and interest in it and then discipline is not the opposite of freedom.

Actually this is the way to find freedom. Then your understanding and opinion about freedom will reach a greater height. Freedom and discipline together are realized as complimentary and rise to a new level of comprehension.

If you don't understand what you are doing then of course you will not like discipline. Therefore having good teachers is important. Then the right understanding and practice can become effective. Everything must be understood via experience.

Sometimes, destructive things are more attractive for people and discipline less so, but by experience you can understand better the need for more discipline. With discipline there is more purity and one can avoid many problems. I think this all depends on wisdom.

The Correct Teachings

Here in Australia there are few proper Tantric teachers. In India there are some who are not known as Tantric teachers, but in reality they are. They can hide and have secrets. There are many features in Tantric practice, and in India there are many related publications. In Western society there are simplifications, imitations and deviations in regards to Tantra. Tantra is the essence of Yoga and Yoga properly understood is the highest level of Tantra. It is the way of understanding freedom correctly. In Australia there is a lot of freedom and from one side this is good, but for many they have this freedom but cannot use it well. If someone chooses a certain type of life, say as a beggar, one can say from a Tantric perspective this is neither good nor bad, but a free choice. Tantra is really about intelligence, not about judgment. Tantra is a scientific knowledge and the main idea is that Supreme Being is omnipresent, and that omnipresence is within everything and every activity.

The question is, 'How can the Supreme Being be present in the most immoral person?' We believe this is true because God cannot be here and not there, as if God is allowed only to stay in this house and not that house. God or Supreme Being cannot be separated or isolated. So for instance, in India some Tantrics invite prostitutes and lower caste people to their ceremonies, not because such people will immediately become Tantrics, but some elements of the Puja can help to attract particular energies. They are often not aware of what is happening, but Tantrics try to extend their practices and teachings. All human beings have some spirituality. Every person can extend themselves, their energies, and others can feel some attraction. Here too we have freedom. It is a free choice. God gives us freedom to choose this or that. If someone wants to become a criminal or commit suicide they have that freedom. They can make such a choice or choose to avoid such things. Theoretically everyone can change but it depends much on karma.

We have to actually experience life, not only theorize. For example, I wanted to emigrate from Russia. On the internet it seemed easy but when I actually tried to do it, it was very different. Then I knew for sure whether it was easy or difficult. So finding a purposeful and happy life is difficult for people. In theory it may seem easy, but everyone has a chance. I needed to find an immigration agent who really knew how to perform this task. It needed to be someone who could give the right information and really be of help. It is the same in the spiritual arena. If you can find a proper teacher, who can give you honest and appropriate information about your way, what you can do, then that is important, because sometimes teachers and Gurus care more about money than people. An authentic teacher would not impart teachings or practices for money if the seeker were not ready to receive. If a person asks, 'What should I do?' the teacher should respond honestly. It's like soldiers going to war; they should all protect each other and be very skilful. If there is one who is a weak link it puts all in danger. They should then help the weak one so they can avoid negative consequences.

The point is that one weakness can create problems for everything. So if a Guru takes on a very weak person it can be a problem for the Guru and everyone else. If the Guru makes a mistake all can suffer. This is a sobering fact. If you take people who are not ready with you it can become problematic. Maybe someone thinks, 'No, this is not a problem. It is like entertainment.' Supreme freedom means you should overcome many things in life. Nothing should be wasted or useless.

Appropriate Contexts

I will tell you a story. I witnessed this. A woman, a tourist visited an Arabic country and walked in a public place wearing a mini skirt and someone whipped her legs in front of the crowd. She received deep injuries. After that trauma she developed a phobia and needed psychological help. She was Ukrainian and was out to show her superiority over the local people. She thought, 'This is freedom,' but she didn't understand what appropriate behavior is. Maybe she was making a statement: my culture is better than yours. If she had done this in a Tantric setting there would be no problem. It depends on context, the situation at hand.

One more remark about freedom: freedom should be honest. If one says something and acts differently one should not complain. Freedom should also be responsible. The woman who got whipped wasn't naive, rather she was stupid. One version of freedom is that if one's person's freedom clashes with another person's freedom, a conflict may start. As for stupidity, this is something that is rarely brought up in spiritual books but it is most important. People like to avoid this topic. This is important especially in spiritual matters.

"Why is this avoided?"

I think that many people are dishonest, cheat and deceive others. For instance, if I overly simplify and offer people many things, this would be a form of deceiving. I would be dishonest and therefore cheating, because if we mislead people for whatever reason, for some personal benefit, than this is cheating. I could say this is bad intention.

An example could be, let's say I give some yoga exercises to someone and say this practice will remove your psychological illnesses, or can bring you special powers or eternal happiness, like liberation, superficially without any deep background and wise processes, this would be dishonest. With simple methods you cannot make such promises. There are no such miracles. If someone wants miracles a Guru should honestly say, 'This is very difficult.'

I can explain how a miracle could be, but just a hint. From that hint, that little indication, you would understand it is not easy to experience a miracle.

The real miracle is that God is omnipresent. Sometimes people are naive, they want big external miracles. They have infantile ideas about what miracles are. Such people also ask, 'If God hasn't given you wisdom then how can you give it?' In some Tantric teachings it is written, 'Guru is even higher than God.' Of course this is a metaphor. The truth is we cannot see God. God is super consciousness. The proper corrector and teacher in human form is the one you can see.

Some say if the Guru is within then ask for guidance from your inner Guru, there is no need for an external Guru, but this is obviously absurd when someone is without wisdom. A more honest expression for many would be to say, 'I am not ready to study. It is too difficult. Or I have no interest.'

Some are also naive in thinking that in India there are only pure yogis. It is a poor country so of course there are many deceivers. There are some Tantrics who are into forms of magic. This is spiritual sensationalism.

For instance powers directed against enemies. Even some politicians in India indulge in such practices especially during elections. These deities represent such actions therefore for them it is justified. It's like you have a rich and powerful friend.

Everyone can have similar problems, but some are in a position to help and others can receive help. It is the same if you have a good relationship with deities. Also if someone deserves to be punished a Tantric cannot do the punishing. He can only feel the karma of that person because only the Supreme Reality can punish.

"So the deities are transpersonal energies, some of which are benevolent and others malevolent, and we are free to call on either."

Yes, so you can call on Kali for spiritual liberation or you can ask Kali to kill. It is the same deity. Why should she kill? If someone doesn't like Putin, and asks Kali to destroy him, whose responsibility is that? One should really understand what is right and wrong action.

Spirit and Authenticity

Kali is neutral. She can support people. I'll give you an example. I have a friend who is a businessman in Russia and he is also my student. Before he became my student he tried worshipping Kali by himself, without a Guru. He then lost a few million dollars because he tried an experiment with a Kali mantra. I told him, 'First of all you should study who Kali is. She would tell you about renunciation. How by removing all your property you could become more spiritual. She gave you quick spiritual progress by stripping you of your money.' After he lost the money I told him, 'You should do these practices very carefully and not by yourself.'

Kali is not like dough, something you can play with and make anything you like with. She is a living consciousness: a living entity who doesn't accept stupid jokes. So there are many misunderstandings in Tantra: for example, ritualistic sex or magical happenings. In India many people try to justify their bad behavior by believing karma will punish them, and accept this as penance.

Therefore a Tantric must be sincere, deep and honest otherwise it is not Tantra. It is not enough to understand the techniques, but also situations. A Tantric should develop wisdom and wisdom is related to energy, Shakti. The essential quality of Tantra transcends particular traditions.

Either one belongs or not depending on inner qualities. One of these qualities is universalism. Not just as a label but really being able to embrace everything. A more mature form of universalism includes particularism, otherwise it becomes New Age babble. Universalism as a concept is for spiritual infants. That's fine if they need to think about this but later hopefully they can deeply study it. We can say that much so-called spirituality and New Age fads is infected by glamour, such as, 'All religion is beautiful,' but religion is not separate from general life, ethical and cultural environment and even politics.

One can become pure in body by practicing Hatha Yoga and die from an accident through not being aware of some danger. Listening to ones' intuitions can be helpful. For example, once I stayed in Sri Lanka and one of my students was in Thailand and bought me a ticket to go there. I asked, "Please change the ticket for two days earlier." I didn't know why. I was staying in a house close to the beach. So the flight was changed and whilst I was in the air the Tsunami happened and swept the beaches both in Sri Lanka and Thailand. When I arrived in Thailand my student asked, "Do you know what happened here in Thailand?" I then saw on television the devastation in both Sri Lanka and Thailand in places where I would have been if I hadn't changed my flight. Why did I change my ticket? I followed some feeling. Therefore sometimes we cannot explain such things but there is a feeling.

Sometimes I try to hide the energy of my presence. In Russia, when I sat on the Metro after doing Puja and spiritual practices, I would be sitting opposite people and they would immediately have a strong reaction, maybe like a jolt. I wouldn't be doing anything: just sitting peacefully. I would then reflect back to people their moods. This seemed to neutralize the atmosphere. Reality is both bitter and sweet. We can describe a little about traditional Sadhana, spiritual practice, and how this can be integrated into ordinary daily living. This can give a little direction. How this can operate and work well. We can give some hints.

It is difficult to recognize what has been corrupted in these ancient traditional lineages. In the best of traditional teachings what is shared is carefully considered. Traditions should not be confused with Yoga centers. True teachers transmit ways to awaken. That is the real meaning of initiation. With 'Shaktipat' for instance, there is a real transmission of energy, leading to Kundalini awakening. This is an expanded experience and should be supported. If someone is having a spiritual ego-trip, then the experience will feel incomplete. There will be a lack of clarity. You can have a glimpse into a reality but what is important is that you see this, you recognize this feeling of incompleteness. An example is how to not become proud. But first one must acknowledge pride.

Life surrounding us gives teachings, so if you are creating artificial conditions, for instance, if you are feeling dull, problems immediately begin. Maybe someone is proud but not chronically and there is still some purity in sight, and then you should understand the teachings that help to bring you back to your innate purity. You should let go of the pride or other illusions and change this condition quickly. It is not a problem that one experiences pride, it is a problem when it creates suffering. This is not a superficial moral topic, it is practical. The problem can be when one has over-identified with pride, for instance. When you identify with something you become fixed on it. When you are fixed you cannot survive life. It is not practical. Spiritual practices done properly can help. They are like medicines for diseases. Sadhana can be for chronic diseases. A little bit of something, like pride, is okay, but if it's chronic it will be a life-problem.

Sometimes I could imitate pride for particular people, and then I would let it go, like changing radio stations: just press the button. Of course the same applies if I demonstrate how humble I am. One person said, 'Please don't call me Guru because I am very humble, very simple.' It really doesn't matter what people say. I am a Guru or not a Guru.

One should ask, does this work or not? Is merely playing with the words creating humility? Is it authentic? Humility can also be out of control. Attachment is attachment. Life is changeable so when you are fixed you will be beaten. So Shakti, Life, will give you teachings. Having fixed views about how life should be is also fixed.

A good life gives good corrections. A flexible mind helps.

Near Death Experience

It is another beautiful spring day in Warburton. We are sitting outside a café overlooking the North East mountain ranges. We have met a number of times by now and there is a good rhythm being established. With coffees and teas served Keith is ready, 'So Yogi, please share about that day when your life took a drastic change of direction and you were almost killed?'

I was twenty-one at the time. It was evening and I was walking home after instructing my Yoga class, and I decided to take a short cut knowing it would pass through a dangerous section of town. There were always things happening there. It was dark and icy being winter. Suddenly I heard a woman screaming and went to see what was happening. There were a few guys and a woman who was still screaming. They asked me, 'Why are you here?' I replied, 'I heard something and just wanted to check it out.' While I spoke the woman ran away.

I then walked away, perhaps a hundred meters towards my home, but could hear some running footsteps behind me. I understood that they wanted to attack me, but I didn't turn around. Then their footsteps became quicker and louder and I knew they were close to me and I did a martial art kick, like a karate kick. The guy didn't expect this and my kick floored him. At that point there were four of them. Then another guy attacked me with a knife. It was a dark area and he was hysterically slashing at me. Fortunately I was wearing thick material including a coat and the wounds were superficial. He was slashing at me crazily. He tried stabbing me but I somehow warded him off using my bag. In the struggle he injured his knee and this made him even more aggressive. At some point his knee was so badly hurt that he stopped.

Then some of their friends arrived and suddenly there were about ten of them. It seemed like a crowd. I fell down onto the cold icy ground and they began kicking me. I tried moving my head with the kicks because if I stayed rigid I knew they would do serious damage. Even so they caused fractures both to my head and my spine. There was much blood loss and I almost lost consciousness. My sight was blurred and it was only with great difficulty that I could open my eyes. I tried to use my bag against the knife and it is really a miracle that I survived. One pulled my head back while another put the knife against my throat and said, 'Give me the bag.' I already couldn't hear clearly. The guy with the knife cut my throat and another guy pulled the bag away from me. Then they tried to see what was in the bag. The guy with the knife kicked me in the face. I briefly lost consciousness.

Looking in my bag altered their focus. I regained consciousness and listened to their voices. They were saying there wasn't enough light to see what was in my bag. I couldn't move or feel my body but throughout this time I felt no fear. I wasn't sure if I was alive or dead. There was only one guy guarding me while the others were focusing on my bag. I think they had already found something in my bag and he turned to the others and asked something like, 'What have you found?' It was very slippery and I got hold of his leg and pulled him down and I got up and ran like the wind. I don't know how I did that.

I was broken and bleeding but ran home. They gave chase but after a short distance gave up. They realized I had nothing valuable on me. It was not easy to open my door with the key but I finally did and stepped inside where I collapsed on the floor and lay paralyzed for some time. I still didn't know if I was alive or not. Everything felt peaceful and disembodied. When I opened my eyes I thought, 'This is the same life but I'm not sure if it is the same body or when this is,' as if I was seeing all this without my body.

After I regained consciousness I went to the apartment where my mother lived, for it was nearby. She did not recognize me and was afraid to open the door. My face was severely disfigured and I could hardly speak. After a while she realized it was me and let me into her apartment. My parents then transported me to the hospital.

"Do you think you were actually having an out of body experience?"

That sounds crazy to many, but yes, that was how it was. I had heard many people say 'You are not your body' but now I had experiential proof. This was a real bodiless experience. I moved in and out of consciousness, like waves. Finally the bleeding stopped.

Healing Myself

It was late evening by this time. I had collapsed and became increasingly weak. I forget some of what followed because those waves of in and out of consciousness continued. I was almost dead.

My parents drove me to hospital and the doctor said, 'You will survive but you can forget about Yoga because you have serious injuries, many fractures.' She said I would only be able to do 'shavasana' which is known as the corpse posture because it is entirely immobile and passive. They wanted me to stay in hospital until I became stronger but I told them I didn't want to stay and that I would heal myself. So with some suggestions from the doctor that I didn't really take seriously, and after gaining a little more strength, I successfully insisted that I be discharged and went home.

The stress on my brain was great but I felt that I could heal by yogic means. I used some wormwood tubes like cigarettes to apply acupressure to specific points and followed some recipes from books to heal. I used my muscle's memory but it was difficult because I couldn't move my neck. There was also some spinal curvature and damaged discs. After two weeks my outer appearance was restored. I looked the same as before.

When I next visited the doctor she asked, 'Who are you? What can I do for you?'

I said, 'Don't you remember me?'

She was astonished. 'Oh, this is unusual. You look different. This is impossible.' She couldn't believe what she was seeing.

After a month I began doing Yoga asanas, postures. It was painful but gradually I healed my body. There were still some injuries that would take longer to heal including brain injuries.

A few years' later doctors did a brain scan and discovered two cysts, but by meditating I removed them. Last year I had another scan and they were gone. My brain was healed.

In retrospect I can say it was important that this all happened. I experienced a spiritual death, not a physical death. It helped me deeply consider the physical dimension as being like an illusion. I understood that physical life can suddenly end, like blowing out a candle flame, for anyone, but I was no longer afraid of physical death. I am only afraid of a useless, wasted life.

I knew that I existed beyond the physical dimension and in another trans-physical state. This inspired me to increasingly investigate what is beyond the physical dimension.

At that time I was still influenced by a type of Hatha Yoga that was body-centered; even then it seemed rather glamorous and somehow useless by itself. Suddenly I had an experience that revealed that body-oriented yoga was limited. In India I tried to find some beyond body-centered yoga; something that had not fallen prey to glamour. Glamorous ideas about spirituality now seemed superficial and I wanted something authentic.

When I chose to walk home that evening I didn't really think I would be in danger, despite saying earlier that it was considered a dangerous area. I've changed my mind. If your life is useless that is dangerous. Every second we are dying, every second the chemicals in our bodies are making closure. Therefore it's not good to lose your true nature in any moment. We don't know what can happen in the next moment.

There are different contexts. For instance, I felt what might happen in that dangerous area and yet also felt I would remain alive. What appears as bad events can actually be good. I am still alive. I trust something beyond that helps me and arranges circumstances in my life. This trust was always there, deep down, but came and went in waves. At times it was strong but descriptions are only imitations. I believe that supreme reality knows what I need and don't need.

Keith thinks that 'it' arranged that I would survive because of my important mission.

I think this is right. Sometimes we think something is good but it is bad.

I have met many people here in Australia who are untypical and always have difficulties in life that others don't have. There is a sort of sacrifice involved here.

Some people are very artificial even if they follow some common spiritual path. Even you would know people who are intellectual, but not intelligent and definitely not so wise. They are not humane in their natures. Maybe smart but no purity of their deeper human nature, because they are not interested in understanding other people. They have many prejudices, are self-obsessed and not self-enquiring. A 'natural' person, not engaged with this dimension, is also a type of sacrifice. If you are an unusual and natural person, others will know this and place you into a particular frame.

Sometimes when others don't understand you they have respect. They can worship you because you don't fit into their frames. They can respect you and at the same time hate you. If you become like them, mundane and superficial, then they can approve. It is not that you are demonstrating to everyone that you are different. You can be humble, but people who are not caught in this mundane web are rare.

Of course there will always be different groups of people with different interests. Even in economically prosperous countries there are many suicides, even more than in poor countries. There is an oppositional tension within them and in their external circumstances. They cannot see any meaning or value in life and their souls become poisoned by this cunning, demonic dimension. And such people can think, 'I don't want to be a part of that.' It depends on the level of consciousness as to how people approach these matters.

PART 4

A PLACE IN THE WORLD

We are all immigrants. The only difference is who came when.

Useless and Corrupt

Many children don't like going to school. I always asked my parents and teachers, 'Why should I go to school? Can you predict my future?' They would say, 'You will understand it when you are an adult.' When I was an adult I understood that I'd been completely correct in my childhood: that school is almost useless and has minimal value. School did not describe life accurately.

As a child I was right in my ideas. Everything there was useless except meeting some friends, because I did like a few. I liked their inner natures.

When asking teachers questions, I was never satisfied with their answers. For instance I asked, 'Why should I study German?' They said, 'Because we fought them in the war.' I asked, 'That is the reason?' They said, 'Yes.' My own inclination was to study English, but no, they insisted I study German. I said, 'You want to arrange my life completely opposite to my own preferences. Okay I can pretend to study,' but I didn't inwardly accept it.

When the Soviet Union collapsed, many people with degrees became poor and those who hadn't studied in school became millionaires and billionaires. I was right. They didn't teach me properly about life. I saw how Russia became gradually corrupted and I think this has continued. There are some improvements but not much.

There are a few oligarchs who only care about themselves. The leaders mislead the masses. They don't tell the truth and say, 'We want you to be like slaves, while we live like kings.' The ones who are completely destroying their country tell the majority everything is good. They are rascals. They say, 'We are patriotic' but only damage the country.

All politicians have similar natures but the level of hypocrisy differs. Maybe in Russia they are more successful as hypocrites. They cannot conceal it so easily. It is blatant. They expect the masses to stupidly accept or believe them. They expect that people will be brainwashed, but that is not possible.

Shiva and Shakti

In Sanskrit, Shiva is translated as 'The Auspicious One', but without Shakti he is like a corpse. Without Shakti he would not be auspicious. In many yogic texts it is described that they are not separate. They are always together, like consciousness and matter. Only a supreme omnipotent reality can create such order and harmony as this. This order can manifest in many controversial ways. Only this omnipresent reality can transcend the controversy. We try to adopt this transcendental reality to our limited dimensions, our normal environment and human characteristics.

We experience Shiva via Shakti. Shakti is mother and creates physical reality. Everything human is Shiva. Because of Shakti we have our bodies. Through our bodies we become aware of Shiva, our souls. Our body needs realization of our soul. Shiva is consciousness of Shakti who is our body. Shakti needs our spiritual realization. Therefore they need each other to be complete.

Shiva and Shakti belong together in a microcosmic sense, whilst universe and Supreme Source is macrocosm. In Taoism Yang and Yin is the microcosm and Tao is macrocosm. They are parallel symbols.

The microcosm reflects the macrocosm. When Shakti created the universe from primordial reality, then extended and manifested, the same processes appeared in each form, including nature. If you follow nature you are in harmony with the universe. Individual souls unite with Supreme Source. This is spiritual Yoga.

When the body stays in harmony with nature it is possible because of Shakti, then all nature is supportive like a mother. We have many unnatural things in modern life and everything is questionable as to whether it is good or not. Everything can seem right from some point of view. But one should be careful with this type of idea. We have smart phones and computers and sometimes it is good, but if you are addicted to such technology it can be problematic.

Tantra and Yoga promote the image of complementariness between Shakti and Shiva. Yoga means for things to yoke, to unite and fuse together. One type of union is symbolized as rider and horse. In the earliest Upanishad this context was illustrated. It was the first description of Yoga. The God Yama gave a teaching and said, Yoga is when you control your mind, therefore your senses and body, and in this context it is close to Hatha Yoga because Hatha means 'with force' but another interpretation is union. Senses then are like five horses and the one who sits behind in the chariot is like Consciousness.

Then the description of Yoga passed on to the Bhagavad Gita. In the West where generally people are unfamiliar with terms like Shiva and Shakti this symbolism can be easily related to the recognition of harmony. When there is harmony Shiva and Shakti are always present.

The word 'auspicious' is not a commonly used English word but if you can understand suffering related to unnatural conditions then auspiciousness can be understood in a spiritual context. It is a word that points to a universal and social order and natural conditions. It is related also to the word 'dharma.'

One meaning of dharma is support. You follow an order that harmonises and stays in harmony so that order will not destroy you. Harmony can be universal or social. This too can be Yoga.

Intuitively we like to avoid uncomfortable and unnatural experiences. This does not need an official status. You can be a yogi without any external or official recognition. You don't need a certificate from a Yoga center to be a yogi. You can be more a yogi than even those who teach Yoga if your orientation is towards harmony and avoiding everything that brings disharmony.

This is all very natural and simple.

Meditation and Respect

Meditation is a condition whereby consciousness is calm and pure. Disturbance is the opposite of meditation. By meditation you try to avoid disturbance. One can become aware of disturbance but when you are aware you say, 'I am aware.' First I, and then awareness, but who is aware?

It is important what happens in the core of your nature. Meditation should happen there. Another perspective is that you use disturbance like a tool towards developing wisdom.

Only wise people can allow meditation. Stupid people cannot meditate. You can sit in a peaceful looking posture but if there is no wisdom there it is pretense or hypocrisy. Some demonstrate for others like a performance. That is not meditation. Such teachers only care about how they can use others or for their own prestige. How others meditate properly is not their concern. Such spirituality is reduced to a business. Of course it is good if people naturally help others. In my tradition there is no focus on presentation or too much preaching. Simply, if you support harmony, then harmony supports you, and then you become a teacher because you cannot be otherwise. It becomes your way.

"What about the Mahayana Buddhism concept of 'no self' and emptiness?"

The idea of self would then be an illusion. In ancient times there were competitions between different teachings. They would argue their perspectives against each other. Essentially they were saying our methods are better than the others, but there is a story about Buddha when a person came and asked, 'So the self is not real?' and Buddha said, 'That is correct.' Then another person came and said, 'The self is real,' and Buddha said, 'Yes, that is correct.' Then a student who had heard these two opposite answers asked Buddha, 'Why did you answer in that way.' Buddha said, 'For some people it is more helpful to believe there is no self and for others that there is a self.'

If I think I am the Supreme self then the idea that the self is real is maybe not so good for me, but maybe good for somebody else. It is the same with concepts about God or supreme reality. These differences are only mental. Many people merely want to think differently from others. They want a particular position or shape, a way of asserting their individuality; otherwise if you are shapeless others may think you are useless. Therefore they create artificial personalities. Maybe others can relate to one's persona and hopefully approve. This does not require wisdom. Even religions create simple personas. It becomes like a 'spiritual McDonalds.' I think human society was always consumerist but spirituality is about quality.

I think indigenous culture is different and it's a shame that Aboriginal culture was suppressed. This tradition should be rebuilt as much as possible. It is the background of this country and its real history. Any country without a deep history is not good.

Sometimes history can be traumatic. Australian history is not as difficult as in Russia. Russia in the last hundred years has been painful and depressing.

The worst thing in Australia is the destruction of Indigenous people and culture. It is a real shame that many do not care about the roots of Australian history. I think there is a gradual understanding, of course the same applies in New Zealand and America. I already feel devotion to an ancient tradition but now I am living here I have sincere respect and knowledge of Aboriginal culture and history.

We are all immigrants. The only difference is who came when. What happened in Australia also happened in Russia when Christianity came and destroyed the pagan culture that has now completely disappeared. Here in Australia such destruction is not complete. There are still transmissions of the old culture through art, music, dancing, storytelling and so on. I hope that in time Australia will become the best country in the world. It is young and ambitious. There are many new opportunities. Australia has a promising future.

Resident Status

In order to immigrate to Australia I had to acquire enough points. My friend, Father John, offered to help me. We found out that if I found employment in a rural region I could apply to settle there as a sub-class of visa, but this encountered the barrier of discovering that John's organization did not have an officially recognized religious status to match immigration requirements. I had trusted and hoped in the success of that application so was disappointed. Therefore I applied to the immigration department to be granted a regional sponsored visa.

Despite the disappointment I suddenly found this other route and it worked. In addition I applied to the immigration department for a State sponsorship visa. That could be a condition to apply for a permanent visa. A visa could not be granted immediately but if it was for a particular area it was possible.

I applied to be sponsored by the state of New South Wales. I had to score sixty points and did but it required me to stay there for a minimum of two years. That is a condition for a permanent visa. After one year of being on a permanent visa I can apply for citizenship because I have already been in Australia for five years.

As soon as I get an Australian passport I can travel anywhere. I can travel during these two years but not settle anywhere otherwise I violate the visa conditions and would not be able to apply for an Australian passport. This is all a nervous situation because I have many activities overseas, in Russia and Europe. This is now difficult because I cannot stay there for as long as I would wish. I am well known there and some students would support me to continue activities I've already begun.

Maybe I can arrange activities here in Australia. I could develop Nath Yoga here, as it is hardly known. I may teach some features of Tantra and Hinduism. I have a few followers in Sydney but I try not to do anything too involved. Until now I mostly used Australia to rest.

Australia has helped me a lot. For me rest and meditation is the same. Rest is not laziness and is rather associated with enjoyment, but not a mundane type. This has been like a spiritual rejuvenation. Being here also helps me to understand the minds of people in this country and what I can do for them.

When I become a part of Australia I become a part of everything. Service is then for me and others because of related karmic relationships, I hope good karma. I wish for others what I wish for myself. If I wish sincerely and from my deepest nature then that is most similar to other people.

We all have the same basic nature. It is the superficial and artificial that differs, not basic nature. From basic nature one can immediately feel we are all related. I can then say what I do for myself I do for society at the same time.

Therefore I have shared my experience of meditation.

It just happens. It must be natural.

Yoga in Australia

I was invited to Sydney in 2010 to give talks at a spiritual center. After those talks a few people decided to become private students, but I didn't represent myself like a Guru because there wasn't a clear understanding about such a title. I wanted a more sincere relationship with people. There was a need for sacrifice in order to share my teachings. This was not one-sided. Students should also have a serious interest. I gave simple teachings and I think it worked well. I would explain who the Guru is, what Yoga is.

Traditionally people say I teach Yoga but I am not a Guru. I did not justify the idea of a Guru out of pride, but rather because it is a traditional requirement. In ancient scriptures it states that Sadhana, spiritual practices, should be transmitted by a Guru, and that should be the context in which techniques are shown. This changed when Yoga became artificial and people didn't want to engage deeply. I realized that some people say they want to go deep but actually they cannot, and so I gave simple general teachings. If someone really wanted to practice deeply then I would talk about the relationship between a Guru and student, as it would happen normally in India, but in Australia there are not many like that.

Once I met a Yoga instructor on a train and he became interested in my teachings. He visited me and received a mantra that was helpful for yogic development. He asked to be initiated. It isn't easy to find proper students or Gurus. Yoga is now common on all continents, but for most students there is not enough wisdom. Wisdom is not easily obtained. There is a big sacrifice needed. As with any skill it takes a long time and much experience to refine and improve, and only in this way does one become wise.

Many experiences lead one to becoming very experienced. As with writing a book for instance, so it is with Yoga. Yoga is not just a few techniques. It is a way of life and then your lifestyle becomes Yoga. Your observation and understanding of the world is also related to Yoga. The condition of your consciousness, your heart and nature, are all related to Yoga, and your body reflects this like a sensitive and sensible tool. Yoga is like a wise child one could say, paradoxically.

Some people are wise but senile. The brain becomes wooden. This is an allegory for people who have good brains but they don't work well anymore. Over many years wisdom and compassion can be developed, but conservatism sets in and although this may be good to a degree it is not always a recipe for a happy life. There can be a lack of openness towards nature including one's own. Then there can be a lack of flexibility and flexible means life, always fresh. Fresh means consciousness is active.

Cultural Diversity

All the countries I have lived in have been different. South Korea is an Eastern country but is very westernized, compared to China for instance. It is conservative and nationalistic. They enjoy Westerners visiting and are polite hosts. The culture is strict and materially comfortable. They create a really positive image for foreigners. This is important for them. But it was not appealing to stay there forever. By contrast, Russia is quite unique. It is neither western nor eastern but somewhere in the middle, a strange blend.

The eastern strand is more natural. They have respect for parents and elders. For example in South Korea, each lower grade within the universities bows to the higher grades. I asked my teacher, 'Why is there a hierarchy like this?' He replied, 'Every generation started from the first father, the father of the universe. If you feel respect it is because genetically it is your nature. Therefore you cannot avoid it.'

You know, they are a Shamanic type people. They think like shamans. When you look into their eyes you see something authentic. Some may seem wild but there is some goodness there too. It is a type of natural spirituality. Western minds would consider this type of adoration of older people a form of tyranny.

People in the West tend to converse one to one when in groups. They move from one to another like that. But when in India my western friend, John, witnessed people in a circle, with one person at a time talking to the group without being interrupted, John asked, 'How could we have this in the West?' I said, 'John, it is a form of respectful discipline.'

So some cultural forms that seem strange can be judged negatively, but if you look behind the screen you can discover some positive elements. Big misunderstandings between eastern and western cultures can become opportunities for exciting bridges of complementariness. In all western cultures there is a concept of individualism whereas in Eastern cultures they have a concept of collectivism. There are positives and negatives in both, but when someone from either side becomes egotistical and doesn't listen to the opposite view, there is a block, and when that happens to a nation the population becomes imprisoned.

Russia is in the middle. There can be a tension in that.

When Westerners observe a Guru talking to a group they may think it is disrespectful to everyone, because only the Guru is talking.

When John observed a group sharing one by one without interruptions, he thought it was weird, but you can really hear another person when you stop speaking and thinking. This is meditative or yogic listening. Meditation is a sacrifice. When you sacrifice your thoughts it is what is called 'Satsang' in the East, and this is also a spiritual practice. It is a circulation of energy and real transmission via communication.

Russian culture has become weak because of suppressions in all areas of life. There are good and bad features. There is much naivety and misplaced tolerance of corruption and deceptions. They are politically naive. Corruption is openly displayed. Many people are controlled and pushed down. For instance, the rich like to demonstrate their superior status, like a muscle man showing off his biceps.

In Australia the external show of wealth is not like in Russia. In Russia people do bad things and smile. At least here you have a real democracy and there are opportunities for everyone. A democratic society can help every person to find ways of self-expression, and creating things of value for the whole society.

India is quite special. In my opinion many western Indologists have a false picture about Hinduism. One French Indologist, who is considered an expert and has written many books about India, told me this too.

There is a tendency to over-simplify. The colonial powers, such as British and Portuguese, tried to control and make Hinduism less flexible than it naturally was. When religiosity is naturally 'rich' it is difficult to easily comprehend. That wealth can only be accessed by personal surrender. Western scholars study Hinduism but without sufficient personal development or without sincerity. For instance, their ideas about surrendering tend to be individualistic. Therefore they create illusions about the true status of Hinduism.

Understanding is impossible without surrendering. If you study a particular subject and become a professor, it doesn't always mean you have a deep understanding.

India is an ancient and vast culture. Even one lifetime is maybe not enough to understand what is of value in India.

Australia and Globalization

What do I think about Australia? I think this is a very open country because it is young. Youthfulness is always open for many opportunities. The young always have a future. America is quite young too, but not younger than Australia.

Australia is also an ancient country but in the context of its first European settlers and immigrants, it became a multi-national and multi-cultural environment, and this can create special opportunities.

Globally this is an information age. The internet is a huge part of this. Maybe about twenty-five years ago people began to especially think about quantity, but at this point in time it is very important to think about quality. If Australia can care about quality then they will know what they are doing and can become number one. I hope this can happen, and can be my personal contribution. For instance, I have seen here in Australia how there is freedom for all religions to flourish, therefore quantity is here and quality can now improve.

Then we come to the topic of consumerism and this can have a few meanings. Firstly, if you consume something but don't care much about the quality of it, it is like eating junk food. The Australian economic system is not so bad, compared to India and Russia. A good economic system can direct part of their money towards science and culture and that is beneficial to Australia. This creates its own character and faith in itself. It is my belief that Australia could be the leading country in the world, even more than America. It is possible.

Authentic scientism cultivates accurate knowledge, and is concerned with quality: quality of food, and everything actually, quality of mind. Therefore education should be excellent. Teachers should be wise.

Nowadays many international students come to Australia. That is big business. Students pay money to get a permanent visa or a qualification they can take back to their country, but not for knowledge. That is not good. I would like for such students to also care about intelligence. The standard of education here is not too bad but it could be much better.

I have travelled a lot and still pursue that idea for the future. Travelling to many countries is a passion and mission for me. In a year I hope to obtain Australian citizenship and that would afford me more opportunities to travel without having to go to Embassies and apply for visas.

I want to deeply explore different cultures. The spirituality of each culture is related to their general lifestyle and I would like to teach people in Australia about my experiences. I am already doing this but there is room for great expansion.

I have everything now except the one problem regarding visas. It is extremely important for me to be able to freely travel everywhere and contribute to Australian culture in that way. This is a part of my calling.

It is difficult to speak about another culture if you haven't been there. I've listened to many Europeans saying things about Russia, very primitive ideas such as bears in the streets. Or it could be about Australia, that there are kangaroos in every street, or India is only about the Taj Mahal.

As for globalization, I don't think that is always bad. I have a cosmopolitan mind. If you can experience many worldly things then you can decide what is best. If globalism is only about profits and power, like McDonalds, who are not interested in higher values or food, that is bad globalism, but if you provide the environment with improvements to the quality of life, then globalism can be a platform for a creative and kind culture. In this context it is important to have a broad mind. If you can combine depth with globalism then it is good. If not then people become stupid.

Many people wrongly understand depth. They think it is some form of intellectualism and leads to a dry mind. But if you develop a broad and deep mind, then unique opportunities occur that otherwise remain hidden, and then a sincere quality emerges from the sub-conscious. Sub-consciousness is the potential of your consciousness and this is the gateway to self-realization. You can realize many things in life but deeper things remain hidden. Hence a spiritual student should invest energies in that way and be sincere, and combine personal realization with being happy. This is the way to find what is missing.

People are afraid of realization. This is paradoxical because realized people are satisfied. Satisfied people are open and peaceful. If you are at peace your mind is open. People can be afraid of awareness because in awareness illusions about who they are will vanish. They identify with particular characteristics and believe there is security and safety in that. But life is unpredictable. Life is always changing. You cannot stay in one position and be safe. That is why flexibility is important. If one is inflexible it can cause a lot of suffering.

There are many opportunities but not everything has value. Therefore doubts have a place but without chronic paranoia. Not the type of doubts that can lead to depression. General life can bring yogic questions. Buddha came to Yoga by way of his general life.

All leaders of religions and spiritual branches had awakenings because of doubts and questionings. Ordinary social people became yogis. This was because life was a bitter experience as well.

People always try to avoid suffering but suffering pursues us everywhere. This unstable situation surrounding everyone invites us to check our inner state of being: our thoughts and feelings and ask, 'Are they right or not?'

Sometimes we hook into a belief and think it is helpful, but on deeper reflection realize it is not. Other times we may prefer to remain naive, but a yogi cannot be naive. Many believe that naivety is natural. Natural and ignorant are not the same and being an ordinary person, if that means being a simpleton, is unwise.

Ignorance is when you have no doubts. Doubts are important when they increase the quality of our exploration. These kinds of doubts are good, but if doubts are entangled with strong prejudices that can also be ignorance. For example someone may say, 'Chakras don't exist.' Materialistic science cannot ever confirm chakras, but many do not explore even materialistic science. They find a specific fact and then generalize. Some scientists like to avoid controversial topics. They want to belong to the tribe that has doctor's degrees but without deep exploration. They care about titles and grants.

"How do you perceive the need for radical change, and what needs to happen for a shift to occur for humanity and our planet?"

This is a big question, maybe even number one at this moment. We can talk about businesses and corporations that exploit people by way of consumerism in very unconscious ways. A group of people who become powerful and control the powerless understand the things I say. My approach doesn't just help a few people. This is a western democratic country, and I want to help the majority to be aware. I am not here to awaken special elites.

Being born in the Soviet Union, there were many bad things happening, but the idea of equality was essentially right. Nowadays the oligarchs have golden lavatory bowls. This is stupid. We are humans who can die at any moment. These oligarchs have much land, but when they die they will only own two meters, enough size to inter a coffin. If you own many material possessions it can be a very painful death.

I want to support people in not being so naive, understanding the value of their lives and developing self-respect without ego. One should protect oneself from the ravages of a consumerist society. Have an eye for what is truly valuable that supports your health and consciousness.

Such wise ideas may not seem like Yoga but who knows what Yoga is? Yoga is not just doing asanas. It is a science of thinking. Yoga helps people to be aware in life. By this approach they can avoid a useless life with useless situations, situations of being victims of aggressive marketing and consumerist addiction.

Atheism and Dharma

Let me express a little about atheism. Atheism is not necessarily bad. I have met many atheists in Russia including my parents and many friends. The Soviet Union was after all an atheist country. I therefore discussed with many atheists; many people who don't believe in official religions or spiritual organizations or doctrines. They have no confidence in such activities. They don't like the hypocritical environments that they perceive there.

I would ask, 'So you don't like ideas of God?' and they would say, 'I have no evidence of God. I do have evidence of human suffering and enjoyment. I have evidence of human liars who cheat others. I also have evidence of spiritual exploiters and liars. This is the evidence I have.' I would say, 'If you have no evidence of God you cannot say God doesn't exist. You should be honest and say, 'I don't have evidence.' And that's it. If you don't want to explore this you should honestly say, 'I am very lazy. This is a weakness I have.' If you are really honest you cannot say 'I am an atheist.' Also it is possible that spiritual people disappointed you, but that is no reason to not explore many deeper religious topics.

Religious topics are intimately related to cultural matters. In India, for example, many people say that religion represents dharma? Dharma meaning universal, natural, cultural and social law: and how this governs morality. Even the deities represent these dharmic laws but few realize this.

Most people's ideas of God are as a supreme presence that somehow influences and guides general everyday activities, even the most mundane, so that by way of supreme Grace they can protect themselves. They can say this is energy that helps me, so their psychology is that their energy is related to their karma. If you study this deeply you can understand and there is nothing controversial, and then you can be a religious person but not in a primitive and naive way.

We are in different times now. Modern people don't like primitivism. They don't like it when religious leaders treat people like sheep, like stupid animals. Atheism can then be like a tool that can help to develop consciousness and this can be valuable, but like any tool it can also be a weakness. It can be an inflexible impediment. If I use a sincere atheistic approach to research the mind, it can be good. Why not? In this sense a yogi can be an atheist. To simply say, 'I don't believe' can be a form of ignorance. Some atheists think by not believing it is wisdom but it isn't always so. It can be in a particular situation and context but not always, but my point is that something positive exists in atheism. Even atheists can come to me. Humanism leading to compassion can also be a form of atheism.

Integrating Qualities

Compassion and pain are not the same. For instance, if someone has a drug addiction and asks the doctor, 'If you are compassionate then you should give me drugs.' But if this doctor knows that if his patient has more drugs he could die sooner, then how are we to understand compassion in that moment? Compassion is not an excuse to behave crazily. Compassion needs to be accompanied by wisdom. In Sanskrit the term 'bodhichitta' is special. Chitta means consciousness and bodhi means awakened. This means to have a living consciousness. It implies a deep understanding of what I am doing. Therefore I do not suppress in the name of compassion.

There is a New Age compassion that is sentimental and shallow. With Bodhichitta you would understand people. I think high spirituality often combines controversial themes, for example, religion related to heart, love and nature, but this can be perceived as the opposite of knowledge and general education. In reality it is important to combine all of these.

Knowledge without heart becomes dry. It becomes dead knowledge. Heart without a calm mind becomes animalistic. But in modern society it is rare to find heart united with mind. There is a tendency to have only intellectual approaches but both are important.

If you have broad, natural capacities then compassion will be properly experienced and acted on. There will be accurate understanding and an intuitive knowing of how to help others. Otherwise, one can become overly 'missionary' and focused on converting others without any responsibility for their continued welfare.

What can happen if others use wrong ideas? This means genuine caring. I can simply help people become awakened. They already have this capacity. I can help to awaken their wisdom but they already have this wisdom. With wisdom comes responsibility. People must learn to be responsible for themselves.

If some people claim to be devoted to me but they have hidden doubts they cannot claim this. Some small doubts are good but not fixed doubts like prejudices. I just wish that people were not stupid. Stupid people are fodder for those who will deceive them. If I cheat, my reputation will become tainted the following day. This is instant karma. Some people prefer to be stupid. They like it. In that case I say, 'If you don't want to have responsibility for your life I too cannot take responsibility for you. If you want to be lazy it is your choice.'

People often complain about their circumstances, but do nothing to try and change them. Many in Russia complained. So either emigrate or improve life in Russia. Invest your energy in another culture or in this one. Take responsibility for your choices. Do not sleep. Be more aware of activities that are possible. Be as honest as you can be.

Honesty is a big topic. This word is used to give direction so as to explore tendencies. It is not possible to easily explain the meaning of a word like honesty. Books can help a little bit and then you can use it in your real life. A book can be like a candle; it gives fire to another candle. The candle can support this fire. I give only fire.

Maybe some people will read this book and come to you and be interested in meeting me and we can discuss more. Respectful conversations are important. Maybe we can have live conversations in front of an audience and then they can ask questions. We could explore a topic such as honesty. This is much more of a living interaction.

Keith has brought different people together in this way through a harmony festival. This is a way to bring some essential elements to the world, including honesty. He even has the idea of a combined Interfaith book containing a Catholic Priest, a Buddhist Lama and myself. Maybe that can happen at a later time. This is an excellent idea.

I too want to fill a void that exists in Australia. Unlike America there is a vacuum here, a great external emptiness that is also an opportunity for the future. Australia is cautious about who settles here. This would be good if it was wisely directed and not fuelled by stupid paranoia. I have seen those tendencies here too. If Australia aims for the best quality in everything then there is a positive future.

An aggressive nature is not symbolic of real power. It is rather a symbol of stupidity. In Tantra the total external world is fused with the internal, and you can be aware of this experientially and then make corrections.

You can heal inner conflicts and create inner harmony that is a part of your nature. When one element becomes larger than another disharmony happens, then a rebalancing can occur and external harmony can be achieved from inner harmony.

Jatis

Childish people, not child-like as Jesus mentioned, but immature like the ignorant Fool in the Tarot, are like people who understand nothing. That is a negative zero. Not a wise zero.

The Indian caste system illustrates some interesting related aspects. This is complicated but worthwhile to investigate.

In olden times there were 'Jatis', jati is now translated as caste. I think the Portuguese invented the word 'caste' but earlier the term was jati, from the root Ja that means birth or 'that which is born.' Previously jatis were related to a particular type of birth and work. For instance, one's father may have been a craftsman with good skills, having developed these over his entire life and he passed these skills lovingly onto his son. The father transmitted all his knowledge and skill to his son.

Compared to this, when someone passes something onto others there is no coherent way of knowing where the knowledge is going, if anywhere. Nowadays people can be trained and you can be their employer, but there is no deep relationship, so the employed one may betray you.

Therefore in ancient India it was thought that it was unlikely that a relationship between father and son would include betrayal, the same between mothers and daughters. Maybe it was possible between others to have a respectful relationship back then like teachers and students, but the teacher was regarded as a father. Westerners didn't understand the old Indian system. It was viewed as too fixed. For example, what if I belonged to a family of craftspeople and I wanted to be a translator? If I'd never studied English it would take many years to become proficient enough to change my job.

Maybe my general activities change, but if I have been a craftsman all my life and achieved fame because I was good at what I do, then people like me because I work very beautifully and professionally. They think, 'He has perfected his craft and the quality of his work is of a very high standard,' and you take enjoyment from this, and you make a good living from this, and you can support yourself and your family, this is all related to your survival and to your relationships with those close to you. Well, it was like that for many years in India.

All Eastern societies have a similar structure. This was more closely related to children learning from their families rather than schools. Many countries, when they become independent become very poor, so this also happened when India gained its independence.

Can we really say this is independence? Independent maybe, but politically corrupt with their hidden overseas bank accounts and properties. I am not rich so my perspective is different from theirs. These are oligarchs who create their own situations. Therefore they control others, even whole societies and countries. Officially a country might be independent but practically it is still like a colony.

India became independent but corruption continued and many do not care about their culture or the enslavement of the population. The elite still rule and from the time of independence education became more westernized and the old traditions were increasingly discarded. They accepted professions not according to family skills, and this way became blocked. Now you can see Brahmins sweeping roads and lower skilled become politicians. Now everything is mixed.

In the old way when parents transmitted to their children it was related to genetics and rebirth. Rebirth was associated with choosing your parents according to the previous life. There was karmic coherence related to a continuum of growth and learning. This was the real law of attraction. What you didn't learn in one life you could in the next. You would attract that which you hadn't understood yet. This was the background of spiritual relationships because it was embedded in your soul, and it was also genetic. It was all naturally related and ordered.

So you cannot say this was a meaningless system in India. Indeed it was extremely logical. I understood this when in India. When I first began to study Indian topics I thought the caste system discriminates, but then realized this is a western interpretation.

You know even before independence it was possible for someone to change jobs, but it was also understood that it was not easy to move from one position to another. It would take years and it would involve a change in your nature. This is not just a superficial shift. When you have invested so much in one type of work then decide to change and want to reach the same level of competence it is complex and takes appropriate time.

Most thought it was better to improve the capacities you already possessed. Even within one profession or job you can develop a range of skills and influence others. So how can you find your dharma, your natural purpose? You can find it related to your job. What can you do in the best way? What do you really like? Then aim for excellence.

PART 5

TANTRA

To be successful in Yoga it helps if you understand the essence of Tantra.

Beyond Depression

We are sitting around the table, the four of us. Keith has a question.

"What about people who don't want to do a job they have no feeling for, but feel they have no choice because it is their survival? Or others who don't want to work at all? Many people in today's world are either jobless or doing work they have no feeling for. This is surely not their dharma. It is survival."

My student responds, "It's not only to survive. They go to the office, get some money and spend it on things they desire to have."

My view is that such people are on the way to discovering their dharma. They are still trying to find their dharma and this is a process. They are approximately finding their dharma including discovering what it isn't. There is already some result. If someone really doesn't find anything, then they are just starting on their journey.

It is not always related to money. Some people have much money but do nothing, like a jobless billionaire. In that case his dharma is related to an inner plane. Maybe they must explore themselves. What topic do they want to direct their minds to? What topics attract them, their consciousness?

Everyone uses time and energy for something.

What do I think about depression?

There are people who doubt everything. Even if they have been flooded by information and teachings of every type, they doubt it all and in a way they are correct. From one point of view life is a big illusion. It is true the mundane dimension is full of illusions.

Such people lack authentic spiritual knowledge, which they could get from meditation. There are not enough inner discoveries, and according to traditional understanding, depression happens when one becomes too engaged with externalities.

When one delves deeper inwardly, one can find many illusions and imbalances and try to be slippery in avoiding them, slip around and not really face them. We cannot blame these people. Some are intelligent but don't like being more natural. They might read books and receive much information but are still confused. They can be in a destructive atmosphere. There is a teaching that responds to this.

We should engage in directing our attention towards 'Atman', our supreme self, because there cannot be suffering there. Where there is suffering it cannot be you. They should try and understand Atman, our supreme self. But of course this is not easy.

A wrong understanding of spirituality doesn't help. One must always strive for a purer understanding therefore of course it is difficult. It is difficult but at the same time, the simplest. This is the paradoxical situation. True surrendering is impossible even though some like to imitate.

In Sanskrit there is the word 'Tyaga' which means when you let something go, but with a feeling of sacrifice. This is related to the sense of leaving your desire behind without care. Tyaga means leaving something because of a particular aim, like surrendering something lesser for something greater: surrendering an ambition, for example. It is a sacrifice, because it is surrendering an attachment to something. If this is not my glass I can drop and break it and it doesn't matter, but if it's mine it matters. Whatever I own and feel attached to, it is a sacrifice to let go. If a computer belongs to an enemy and it breaks I might be happy, but if it belongs to me it's quite a different situation. If you are attached you are dependent and not flexible. When I am thinking this is my glass and my computer I'm always in fear. This fear contracts me and I can't be open to new opportunities, and maybe a new computer.

There should always be some space. If I hold things with both hands I can't pick something else up. One hand should be free. To be effective I should always be in Yoga, in an empty condition. One meaning of Yoga is emptiness and also union. In union there is balance, a natural stability. This table, pizza, glass and sugar: all are related and are in union. To be flexible I should be aware of the whole picture.

Without Yoga I cannot be in perfection and successful. Siddhi means success. Without an aware yogic condition it is like driving a car, when it is necessary to be aware of everything happening around you, otherwise you are in danger. Do not exceed the speed limit because a camera may catch you. Being alert is yogic awareness. In this way Yoga is knowledge of survival. Animals use a yogic nature according to the consciousness of the animal. Humans are also animal but developed in a particular way. Buddhists would say that enlightenment is within all sentient beings. Every creature has its own unique nature, but humans have a developed capacity for self-reflection.

Dharma and Anti-Dharma

Dharma means support and can also be translated as 'order.' Everything is in a particular order and supports other things. Animals follow their own dharma. You can find some people like that; they don't deviate from their natural dharma. We cannot say that all humans deviate from their dharma. A tiger may want to kill a person but doesn't have a perverted mind, but some humans kill because they have perversions, so it is true that animals in that sense are purer than these humans.

Perversions are anti-dharma and lead to suffering. Some people have become like maniacs. It could be said that such people are worse than animals. There is a great spectrum of behavior and consciousness within the human species. Another perspective is that yogis are like the enemies of normal people. Many people don't know what they are doing. They can do destructive and crazy things. They are ignorant.

From one angle it can seem freedom and democracy are very good, however not always, because they create confusion. It really doesn't matter what people refer to themselves as, or what their systems are, whether communist, democratic, capitalist and so on.

These are only external masks and a shift from one to another is only ever superficial. The illusion changes, the external decorations become different. Russia is a good example.

Under communism it was said they believed in the equality of people, but it has never been like that. The aim is therefore to change the consciousness of people, but this is a difficult topic. One aspect concerns the atmosphere of our development.

With freedom comes the temptation to become increasingly lost. For instance, you can be enticed by products in shops, but you don't have to buy. You can buy by using the mind wisely because there are many traps in consumerism, and illusions of independence. A child might blame the parents for not buying more toys, but they spend the money for food or renting a house, but when the child is young he may not understand. He thinks this is a big disaster. 'I want more toys.' Many adults are like that child. They don't know what's best for them.

So God or Supreme Being is like a father who cares for the future of humanity, but many people prefer toys.

Friendship

"What is true friendship?"

The word 'true' is complex. True friendship between two people is possible only when both are travelling towards enlightenment; otherwise both can be seduced and betray each other, not immediately but eventually. For some small profit the friendship can be betrayed. I believe there should be a very high orientation for both, and therefore real friendship rarely happens, but one should not be disappointed when people betray or disappoint us.

There are many artificial friendships. The normal situation is one of people being ignorant because most are unenlightened. We can make a comparison between enlightenment and ignorance because ignorance also exists. Enlightenment is beyond contrasts, so someone can increasingly care about purity and always check him or her-self. 'Am I making mistakes or not?' Such a person can be a friend.

Of course there are other levels of friendship such as those with common interests, but they are always risky and unstable. I could say simple friendships are possible, but I have doubts about that. I think one aspect of friendship is when you can talk about anything without concealment.

It is a sign. This is not a question of morality. Morality depends on variable factors. Morality can be faked. So there is honesty in friendship. Honesty is a foundation for true friendship.

Gorakhnath is an example of someone who is always alone and doesn't need friendship. He likes solitude. He is alone in all dimensions because he can embrace them all and therefore he is free. Why then did he share this with other yogis? Actually he didn't, it was just his normal condition, and he helped by simply being in that way. He wasn't presenting teachings for his own sake, and people were naturally attracted to him.

Krishnamurti

Krishnamurti was Keith's first teacher in this life.

"Actually this is not quite accurate. He was the first who awakened me to the depth that was dormant until then."

I think some of Krishnamurti's ideas are nice, but he also criticized all Gurus. He said there is no need for Gurus. Some people cared very much for him but then later he just left them behind when he became famous. For me it is not good to behave like that. Many people liked Krishnamurti but if we don't need Gurus then why make your organization with yourself as head? Even if you say 'I am not a Guru' but nonetheless you are a leader.

"It's true. Krishnamurti did take an anti-Guru position. He was obviously a leader as you say Yogi, but he tried to engage his audiences in a type of mutual process of enquiry. He encouraged an audience to enquire with him."

But why did Krishnamurti sit above on a chair and others below him if he is not a Guru? If you do not accept the concept of a Guru then why behave like one? Some Lamas also sit on thrones and say, 'We are equal.'

"For me Yogi, Krishnamurti was an example of someone who continuously shared the message, 'Think for your-self and stop being a slave to others.' But he was human too and may indeed have had weaknesses and blind spots."

I believe he helped in many ways. If some people came to me and said, 'We all have an inner Guru.' I would say, 'If you don't need an outer Guru why are you coming to me and asking very technical questions? Ask these questions of your inner Guru or directly from life.' To say you don't need a Guru is then a sleight of hand. I would be careful in accepting his ideas. Why should one thank ordinary people but not a Guru? If everyone is the same then there is no need for gratitude, but this is a false idea of equality. Feeling and expressing gratitude is natural.

"If I have a good teacher I respect the teacher for knowing more than I do. I express gratitude because his superior wisdom helps me. This could be any situation. In this sense it is an illusion to say all are equal. Guru is a role or if not he is in solitude. If he is engaging in the world then he has a role and so does the student. If these roles are complimentary then of course there is a difference in inner qualities and outer skills. Then it would be natural for respect and gratitude."

Let us imagine that all Gurus no longer exist so this term no longer exists. However when I talk with someone and he accepts my knowledge what should he do? Or the other way around, what should I do? Should I not say something? When I am silent I can be receptive. If I am very active I cannot listen. Normally I listen to another person when I'm interested because I cannot have interest in something that is not important, and if this is important to me then that is a type of respect. So it is in my nature. I am respecting my own interest too, even some small adoration of my interest. We have this in our sub-consciousness. When I cannot become empty I cannot study. Emptiness is the condition of a disciple but Gurus must also be empty. I cannot understand a student if I think I am very knowledgeable.

My student adds, "There are many Gurus who think they are very knowledgeable and say to others 'shut up.' Just sit here and meditate."

Gurus should be sensible. They should be empty in order to understand people and that is a sort of sacrifice. Emptiness is Yoga. When one says I respect the Guru that is incorrect, it is respecting the Guru conception.

Krishnamurti's ideas are right in one sense, because when Indians go to Western countries they understand that people like ideas about freedom, and they can say I will teach you about freedom, and this message attracts many people. But this quick way to freedom is not really helpful in the bigger picture. Therefore one should be most cautious about believing such concepts. I think a Guru cannot feel satisfied if his students become crazy. If one of my students misunderstands me, I cannot accept that easily.

For Keith, Krishnamurti was not as I perceive him. That's good. My biographer shouldn't have to agree with everything I think or view everything as I do. We can appreciate that and continue to work fruitfully together.

Trauma

Doubts, devotion and everything else related to the topic of spirituality is good depending on context. Traumas are many and are often interwoven. My point of view about trauma is that trauma happens in one's present life, but we do not know the inherited traumas we carry in our deep memories and genes.

Maybe I was an animal and someone killed me. This is evolutionary memory.

Some traumas we don't like to remember. Usually we only want to remember what has happened in this present life, because those memories are still close to awareness. It is difficult to forget them, but there are many traumas we have forgotten. Personally I want to love my traumas and not suppress them. I want to recover them and cannot if I don't accept them.

So acceptance is a step in the process but I cannot accept that which I don't love. When I accept it I can peacefully become aware of trauma without negative feelings. I can only see clearly when in peace. Such a peaceful condition is yogic. This is the meaning of 'Samadhi'.

With an increase of peace you can penetrate into many memories.

Sometimes you don't like to remember. For instance, if you were a mouse and somebody stamped on you, crushed you underfoot. How can you peacefully remember this? It means you would remember strong pain, so there is also a big sacrifice involved. Samadhi is a big sacrifice. You are sacrificing your attachment to your traumatic dramas.

When I was in kindergarten a child stole a toy of mine. This shocked me: that someone could lie and steal. I remember I was shocked for a long time, but when more mature I finally understood that the attachment to emotional pain was preventing peacefulness. I understood I'm not only this body, but also the bodies of all other bodies including all their traumas. This includes all animals.

I should accept all traumas. If I believe that I embrace everything then how is that possible without full acceptance? Some say 'I am Shiva' and so if I am Shiva and this is my creation, how can I not love it? I should sacrifice this limited concept of me and mine: my pain, my trauma, otherwise I cannot feel another. My capacity to feel can become so narrow. I could become very intellectual and say, I am Shiva or I am Brahma without it being a real experience. Even a little real experience can be a shock. Overcoming this threshold of shock can be a difficult process, but is entirely possible. Shiva though, is never shocked.

Many people find themselves in very difficult situations, including some of my Russian friends, some of who were in Chechnya and became crazy. It can be very difficult to recover. There are ongoing disturbances in their behavior and personalities, but life isn't finished, even for them. It is a challenge to be sensible and caring and simultaneously be beyond everything. That is a great art, an art of living, but if you want to evolve there is no other way.

Great Metaphors

Recently I shared with a few of my students in Russia, Puranas, scriptures or sacred texts, where there are sometimes accompanying images of Krishna, Shiva or other deities. For example, once Krishna fought against a warrior, and some of Krishna's blood was spilt, so how could God allow this? Shiva too was involved in some difficult circumstances. Sometimes he had conflicts with Parvarti, like a family conflict. Sometimes one of his children, such as Ganesha, wouldn't listen, with severe punishments that followed.

In the Bible, Satan is sometimes mentioned. Satan does opposite things to God. So why do people not blame God for their troubles? They never ask questions like, if Satan is independent then how can God be omnipotent?

"How could God allow that to happen?"

Like children, people think Satan is opposite to God. I think all these stories about deities are calling out for deeper understanding and in profoundly practical ways. When bad things happen we often doubt our capacities and ourselves. We doubt our positive perspectives. We doubt our supreme self.

"We want to be God without Satan, eh?"

Yes, so when challenges happen in our lives we should not forget that our nature is always supreme and enlightened, even in the worst situations.

"So why did God allow Satan to have such freedom?"

There are many bacteria's surrounding us in the atmosphere. Why does our biology have an immune system? We need it to survive. It is the same on the spiritual level as the biological. It is within our nature and also the universes.

This is not an artificial construct that we should follow nature. How can we become powerful and wise without obstacles? It is difficult but we should be beyond the universal drama. All these stories in the Tantras and Puranas are like fairytales for children, but for wise people they are examples and metaphors. All of life, even the most mundane can be understood in this context.

Interfaith Tantra

I am at an Interfaith Tantric two-day conference in an outer Melbourne suburb, as one of six presenters representing an array of faiths. Keith is here too and is in an audience of about twenty-five. I will be the first to present during the morning, but before that we have been introduced and asked to say a little about ourselves and our approaches to Tantra. I will try my best but am somewhat tired. Mornings are not my best times because I am often awake during the night, communicating with students and others in Europe and elsewhere. And later today I will fly to Latvia to give teachings to my students, and will be away for two weeks, so I spent the early morning packing. Anyway it is my turn to introduce myself and say something about my approach.

'My tradition originated in North India and is related to Tantra. Within Yoga there are also elements of Tantra, like Kundalini and Shakti. In my thinking Yoga is the essence of Tantra. Yoga is therefore related to inner processes. To be successful in Yoga it helps if you understand the essence of Tantra, because Yoga appeared in an environment of Tantra. Of course there are many different types of Yoga nowadays. Yoga is now everywhere but mostly non-traditional. Kundalini is energy in our bodies and an aspect of universal power, the mother of the universe. In Tantra there is worship of the Goddess and an understanding of

how she developed consciousness, and is therefore a personification of supreme wisdom. She needs a partner and that is Shiva. So Yoga and Tantra are focused on the union of Shakti and Shiva. This is just a brief introduction.'

The five other presenters introduced their approaches, and then after a short tea break it was my morning session.

I wonder if it being Saturday November 14th with news of the Paris killings filtering through to us had any significance to my presentation. You can decide.

Father John Dupuche introduced me. "Yogi has a large number of students around the world. He has a website and is well versed in his field, so he will now speak about Tantra."

'There are many Tantric traditions in India, some quite ancient. Shakti, the feminine power, is an essential element in Tantra, one of its main symbols. In the Vedas most of the deities are masculine, however there are some feminine deities, but in Tantra there is great devotion given to Shakti, the universal mother who protects those who worship her. She offers her worshippers spiritual liberation. She is also related to Kundalini. Her universal grace descends and is called Shaktipat. This is an important process in spiritual development and can be initiated by a Guru to the student.

There are many branches of Shaktism, divided mainly into two sections. One is very popular in South India, the other in the North, where they worship the Goddess Kali. These two branches can appear quite different. Kali is the more marginal and is associated with cremation grounds, wine and meat. She is sometimes depicted having sexual intercourse with her consort Shiva. Shri Yantra is the symbol representing the Queen of all the Tantric yantras. She rules three dimensions: earthly, environmental and cosmic. She is full of beauty, light and power. She is Grace and *gives liberation. She has two aspects: one related to light represented by Tripura Sundari and the second related to darkness, which is represented by Kali. Kali is also related to time. Time is always moving and changing. Her color is black and this is associated with death. With time we age and finally we leave this world. If you worship Kali you are related to her destructive powers. This aspect of Kali is the slayer of evil parts of human nature. In India there are special times of purification of these negative parts of human nature, both at the beginning of spring and autumn. Then devotees of the Goddess recite seven hundred shlokas or mantras over nine nights to purify and eliminate imperfections. If you worship Kali you can attain much power and purity.*

The demons are symbols of our human weaknesses. These weaknesses are common human weaknesses such as anger, lust and envy. Many in the West misunderstand Tantra and associate it with erotic massage or Californian-style sexual indulgence. Of course you can find some sexual elements in Tantra that are very meaningful, indeed profoundly sacred and secret: secret because people can misuse these powers. There is already too much misuse like that in Western society. Such sexual rituals are types of Puja or purification. One cannot do such rituals without devotion.

So symbolically Kali kills demons and is concerned with removing our anger, envy and other weaknesses, and finally she leads us to enlightenment. When we discover our purity and support it by our spiritual practices we can remove suffering. Our suffering has appeared from ignorance. So this level of Kali's image is associated with impurity. In India they are very strict about this. No wine or meat, for instance. Many such devotees are vegetarian.

Another example of this type of experience is when you enter a temple or mosque you feel purity as long as you worship. From an ordinary social perspective and living this can all seem questionable. This can become a dilemma. Your purity polarizes against ordinary social consciousness and behavior, but then your purity is limited. Then within this polarity you engage in conflict. This account may be marginal but it can help to purify in a general, broader sense. One can become aware of the power of Shakti and this can be an advanced spiritual awakening. On the lower levels of every religion they don't address this topic, or at least minimally. This is also important because general rules can clear up general purity.

As I mentioned, in Tantra we worship Shri Yantra who is a Goddess of light or Tripura Sundari, so there are two different primal energies. The second is Kali and she is like night time when you can see stars in the sky, where everything dissolves. So she is related to dissolution and emptiness. Darkness is then primordial reality in which all matter appears, such as galaxies and planets, including our world. Lightness is perceived as extremely small and darkness as vast. Sometimes we can feel that darkness is bad and light is good, but they are really complementary. What would happen if the stars disappeared and only darkness remained: that is impossible, because if there was only darkness there could be no light: in either case you could not say 'this is darkness or this is light.' Therefore both these two traditions (Shrikula and Kalikula) complement each other. Together the rituals of both lead to a total awareness of Shakti. There is an initiation that is of fullness of being. There are further initiations but this is the beginning of experiencing Shakti power.

A yantra is an image of a deity, so Shri Yantra is very famous in India. It is a combination of many symbols: many combinations of angles. In the center of Shri Yantra there is a dot. Two triangles surround the dot representing the union of feminine and masculine powers, and the dot is the supreme universal power. This union creates rays that spread and become different Shaktis or energies. The dot in the center also symbolizes 'ananda' or bliss. When those polar angles join there is bliss, therefore it is a most sacred place in yantra; when this happens all the energies of the chakras move to the center. This is creation and dissolution. If a Tantrika wants liberation then the process moves all energies to the center.

In India there are numerous deities because among human beings there are such different characters, and of course yogis and yoginis have different attachments and desires. Normal religion thinks desire is a limitation for spirituality. In Tantra we try and combine desire and spirituality and therefore transform our attachments. In India many practitioners also think that via Shakti they can get mundane beneficial outcomes. These are magical conceptions. In Western society many think Tantra is only about sex: like some form of sexual entertainment. This is a wrong concept devoid of spiritual presence: whereas in India the prejudice is more oriented towards the false belief that Tantra is about secret magical practices. Then the focus is about making money or defeating enemies or getting revenge, like witchcraft with magical spells. There are books dedicated to such type of things both in the East and West. Of course it within human nature to want to grasp at overly simple beliefs but I don't think God is that crazy.'

My morning session continued.

'Imagine you have friends who wield great power socially. If you have some good partnerships that include Yoga, and something challenging happens to you, they can help you naturally, but if you are egotistic and there is some selfish manipulation occurring, the help might come to an end. If you are the recipient of this manipulation and end the partnership, it is because there are some uncomfortable feelings. With deities it is somewhat similar. They are not dumb. Transgressions have consequences and only pure devotion can bring positive results. This is important to understand as you explore and gradually practice Tantra. Even in India if you want to find a reliable Guru it can take time because Tantra is a vast system of knowledge, and is very complex. Some spend a whole lifetime exploring Tantra.

Shiva has five main aspects or 'Mukhas' in Sanskrit: Sadyojata, Vamadeva, Tatpurusha, Aghora and Ishana. For example, Aghora Shiva means fear and going beyond fear. Through this gate all fear is conquered. So in this way all the gates are the five faces of Shiva, representing different human qualities and overcoming their weak aspects. From those five faces, Tantra appears. In Sanskrit the same word 'mukha', can be translated as face or mouth. When Shiva shares his knowledge and power, it is a transmission and Shakti then is Shiva's student, so it is difficult to experience Shiva directly. The fifth gate is in the center of the image of Shri Yantra and symbolizes eternal life. These qualities represented by the gates have been trivialized in Indian culture, for instance, fearlessness is depicted like a Rambo character and this creates a false impression, but real fearlessness is peaceful and calm.

In Tantra by worshipping a power you attain it. You become an aspect of that which you worship. There is a transmission of energy. By identifying with a particular Goddess you take on her qualities.

As with Shakti, Shiva also has many aspects or personifications. In Vedic sources Shiva is described as having five faces that face in four directions, with the fifth facing upwards. In Tantric texts, these faces are also associated with creation, absorption, concealment of the Supreme Being and its revealing. These energies correspond with daily phases of waking up, daily activity, etc. Such phases may vary from three to five.

Adherents face a certain direction whilst reciting an appropriate mantra. Any mantra and direction can work if done properly with devotion. All Tantric deities have consorts and there is union between them. Mudras or sacred gestures are also performed. All these and many more aspects are in the diagram and image of Shri Yantra.'

That of course the reader cannot see as did the audience at the Tantric seminar.

Tantra and Yantra

Tantra is a technique applied by a yogin to transform imperfect qualities into divine ones. That could be described as a type of spiritual alchemy, within which transformation happens. Tantrism is known for its latitude and flexibility of methodology. Developed by Siddha-Yogins, Yoga is the essence of different tantric systems. Mantras and mystical diagrams known as yantras are used in tantric practices during rituals.

Tantra is a skillful combination of multi-variant mantras and yantras. The purpose of these methods is a cultivation of the inner connection between an individual, a mantra with its symbolic deity and all the absolute qualities or siddhis that the deity represents, and the practitioner. A tantra practitioner also leads oneself to realizations of connections between one's body and a mystical diagram or yantra.

By sanctifying a yantra, projecting it onto a physical body and realizing its metaphysical elements that reside within us, we can purify ourselves. It gives powerful energy that initiates us into successfully integrating different aspects of our being: for instance, our inner self as well as our relationship with the society we are connected to.

By worshipping the Mother Goddess (Shakti), we awake 'Her' within ourselves in the form of a mental power of Kundalini. By awakening Kundalini Shakti inside us, we remove blockages in consciousness, emotions, feelings and physical sensations, and begin to see the world more accurately through parallel dimensions, opened to us by this power.

Tantric practice doesn't take the individual away from society. On the contrary, it helps to fulfill all the ambitions in life more adequately. With such a realization a tantric also receives a fullness of spiritual experience, but for this to become more than theory, one must find a decent master, who is willing to teach.

A Guru, by giving a method, also gives his realization pertaining to that method. He also opens the same inborn capacities in a disciple. If a disciple correctly follows a spiritual way, awareness of perfect unity leads to an absolute mutual understanding. The master has realized Shiva's nature within, and through that embodies God and the nature of the Universe (Shakti). A Guru reveals the awareness of such realities within a disciple, which helps the latter to dissolve inner imperfections, such as selfishness.

That many Goddesses in Hinduism are described as human-like is not accidental. It doesn't mean that God is limited and feeble like humans are: rather it implies that God is omnipresent within everything, including human nature. That is why, for example, a Goddess could be mentioned as different ages: a young eight year old girl, a teenager or a twenty-eight year old, or as an old woman.

There are Goddesses that have different manifestations as Shiva's consorts. They could be of any age, for instance, Dhumavati, who as the Goddess symbolizing death and suffering, help us realize the nature of death and suffering in other ways.

All Goddesses of differing ages have their own mantras and initiations that reveal varying levels of spiritual awakening. All of them symbolize different levels of Kundalini-Shakti awakening, and an age of a Goddess corresponds to the number of syllables in a particular mantra.

In the same manner, we consider Shiva as differing forms of Bhairava, a God who transforms various impurities of human nature. But generally, Bhairava represents our consciousness that as with fire encounters and embraces different experiences, until consciousness expands to its original state. This is the highest primordial state, which is forgotten by ordinary people for some reason, but it is possible to remember figuratively and metaphorically. It can be re-opened through tantric practice. In Yoga, such practices are described as Samadhi or different types of deep immersion into inner self.

Methods can vary, but usually I give the easiest and more comprehensible for most who visit me. I suggest practice to include mantra chants and to concentrate on particular centers of the body.

Another View of Tantra

Keith wants me to give another view of Tantra based on the final part of my talk at the Tantric Interfaith Seminar. So I start to talk.

The image of the sky associated with and supported by consciousness that contains the entire objective world, becomes more liberated and flexible. It is a complete state of unifying emptiness (shunya) and fullness of the manifested world (purnata). All this is connected with our individual consciousness, which is a part of super-consciousness (Shiva).

In this context natural Shakti is associated with movement, changes and world transformations. This is important for survival because if you are inflexible unnatural destruction happens. There is a moment when changing from one side to another, for instance, is natural, like the moon suddenly appearing in the night sky, and not being flexible in that moment would be going against the natural order. This is another angle of Tantra: being flexible enough to follow natural change.

With introjection Tantric energies of Shakti flow into your body and you become like Shri Yantra. Our gross and subtle substances, elements in the body (microcosm) have connections with the main elements of Shri Yantra. The body then becomes like a microcosmic fractal of the universe, including the subtle body, which then becomes protected. There are a few initiations in this Tantric process. I can give an example of how it exists, for instance, in Shri Vidya Tantra.

This imagery also relates to an understanding of stages of development or different symbolic ages of Shakti or Goddess: for instance, the Goddess may be young and a virgin. She may be only eight and in India therefore, some worship virgins, who are symbols of the awakening and blossoming energy. This is a stage of initiation known as Samanya-diksha (primary or general) but like a child this initiation is incomplete. Shakti at this stage is virginal and very pure, but she is in need of development of greater wisdom. Children are quick witted and curious about everything. This is a first initiation and there is a mantra for it that is named Balasundary-mantra.

If your development is good the energies go easily to the center, or if not there are blockages. These blockages are karmic suppressions and signs that consciousness is overly mundane and dependent. So prescribed spiritual practices become ways to clear the channels and unblock energies.

When Shakti power joins with Shiva one becomes symbolically an adolescent, about fifteen years old. In India they think there is a beginning of a contact with 'impurity' that sometimes makes people wiser at this age. Shakti becomes inter-operable with 'the impure world' and is capable of transforming it into the nectar of knowledge and divine wisdom. It is the beginning of female bleeding and during these days in India, women are not allowed to cook at that time as well as many other rules. This is the second initiation associated with another level of Shakti awakening. At this stage, some of the sadhaka can practice the ritual related to five sacral pleasures known as panchamakara.

These impure elements are mixed with purity: impure elements 'sacrificed into the fire of consciousness' and become themselves the fire; therefore in Tantra, as opposed to Vedic interpretations, they are called pure. With Tantric initiation the message is that at this stage some impurity exists but it is preferable to those who avoid such encounters. In Tantra it is pure elements that are most important. They are used in special purification practices and rituals. These are stages of the deepest awakening of consciousness.

The belief is that Shakti is of a higher stature than Shiva so Shiva is depicted as a corpse under Shakti's feet. Shiva worships the Goddess, Shakti, so sometimes Tantra Shakti is considered higher than Shiva, thus it is written in Shakta-tantras. The corpse of Shiva is not really dead: rather he is dying so that Shakti can live. Death is a transformation to a new level of life; therefore, the 'death of Shiva' is also another kind of awakening. The diminution of one is the awakening of the other but really they are a complimentary union, like Yin and Yang in Taoism. Shiva sacrifices himself to Shakti and vice versa, so those both rise and reveal their nature. In the context of multi-levels of experience and reality the dissolving of one level is the empowering of another level.

Both Shiva and Shakti have many manifestations represented by many Gods and Goddesses. This can be envisaged as stages of dissolution until reaching the formless union with Supreme Reality. Initiation stages continue associated with various ages of a human being, each stage less mundane and more spiritual. With each stage the mantras get longer. When the mantra becomes as a sixteen syllable mantra there is dissolution of consciousness as Brahman dominates. So at twenty-eight years there are twenty-eight syllables within the mantra. It is quite complicated with a lot of rules. It can take a few years to learn and practice these procedures.

There is the physical level of human life that is the same for everyone. Then there is the spiritual level but we cannot immediately jump from physical to the formless state. We have our physical senses and are attracted to a lot of objects, and among these some dependences. This is what happens to our consciousness. It is called sanskaras in Sanskrit. There are many desires and this is also happening in our subtle bodies. When we have many dependencies we exist in a suppressed condition. So we should clear the subtle levels in order to progress to the spiritual.

The shift from physical to spiritual cannot be made directly for most people. Great yogis can move directly between these states. This all depends on individual karma. First of all we should develop flexibility. Gradually one moves into spiritual levels of consciousness. Spiritual practices are therefore important. Periods of meditation are good, concentrating on the Atman, the natural self. It is possible to become realized in one second.

Choice and Practice

Following the Tantric Interfaith Seminar I visited Europe for two weeks where I met with students and others but most importantly with my beloved Guruji.

About a week after returning to Warburton I resumed meeting with Keith with the intention to complete this biography. Together with one of my students, we set off towards a favorite café and on arriving sat in the summer sun. We settled into the charming riverside garden and ordered light refreshments. We are nearing the end of our time together.

Keith wants to explore what is most important to consider in one's precious human life. He sees two different perspectives about choice. One is that it doesn't matter in the big picture, because whatever one chooses the universe will find its own balance. The other is that every choice has consequences and karma is simply the flow from past through present into future governed by choices we make.

So Keith is now in a dialogue with me. He begins. "Whatever choice is made a lesson is learnt. Humans have free-will and can choose freely and whatever choices are made, will lead to connected consequences.

But to think that in the big picture it doesn't matter what choices I make, robs one of any responsibility. Then nothing really matters and there is no purpose to anything. It means I can do anything I choose. There is no moral dimension present. Whereas the second perspective implies that choices do matter. Can we talk about this Yogi?"

Yes, it is important. Every person incarnates with a specific task and related challenges, lessons and an unrealized general state of being. This unrealized condition leaves a type of heaviness of heart, an uncomfortable feeling. I believe many people feel this way, a sensation that something important is incomplete and a deep happiness is out of reach. At the same time this is entirely personal, and yet equal for everyone. There is a common underlying element but one cannot say that the personal level is insignificant, because they are inter-related. We have something essential in common that we try to understand.

There are many bitter and sweet experiences that appear and disappear, sequentially and intermittently, but with an incomplete feeling. Of course, people have much freedom to explore. There is time to investigate and experiment. We all engage in such investigations. Eventually a breakthrough can happen. Many things can occur in life that is altogether coherent and meaningful when this essential understanding takes place.

Some rare people incarnate already realized. We cannot see what happened in their past incarnations, but we can observe they are very unusual, happy and possess powers. Not many people can be like a Buddha but they potentially have such capacities. They are not fully realized yet, and need to be awakened. There are yet complications and entanglements, like knots. Their minds and souls are cloudy, and this cloudiness is nearly always associated with bitter experiences. It cannot be avoided.

Keith adds, "With the strongest knots they feel they cannot escape, for instance with addictions."

It is like trying to escape from a submerged submarine. What to do? They try to escape but the way out, to begin with, needs to be a very careful investigation of the opportunities and possibilities present. There are a lot of possibilities surrounding us. This is not a bad thing even if this is partly cloudy. It is not black and white. It is multi-coloured.

"So we can't judge simply from the surface manifestation. If someone is feeling desperate and seeks help and comes to a charlatan who is mostly after money, and who says 'Pay me and I will free you from your suffering', but even then something good could come of it, is that what you are implying?"

Partly, everyone can give you something or help you take a step on the big stairway, but it is indescribable and unpredictable. Which way of climbing the steps should it be? If there is a supreme eternal element behind this changeable life, an omnipresent reality, then how can we talk about particular sequences? For each person it must be a unique process and therefore unpredictable. You should be ready and aware of the unexpected, including possibilities you wouldn't like to happen.

Sometimes we must be aware of our ignorant condition and the dark part of our nature. We shouldn't just be aware of our more glamorous spiritual persona. So some methods can be helpful.

"How do I know that a method is good for me?"

There are many questions like this. It is really contextual, different methods for different times. Right context is only acceptable for this moment. Tomorrow it may not be effective because life has changed. Therefore one could ask, 'How many methods must there be?' It is impossible to say. The best methods are related to awareness, grace and wisdom. You ask about a quick method that can be used anytime. Such a method is always needed but that implies a different level of consciousness and is potentially controversial, actually controversial if you have a particular type of psycho-physical development. If something extreme happens inwardly or externally, then a quite different experience can occur. Such experiences can easily be perceived as crazy from a more ordinary perspective. It could seem crazy, incoherent, confused and so on. Again we have context. Today the need might be go without food for a day and next week having sex and alcohol might help. It is personal and contextual. There can be many ways, some very strange, that can help to bring balance.

Sometimes one needs to avoid interactions with others because it would be distracting and other times the need is to be very socially open. So you can be insular when needed in order to be inwardly calm and peaceful. But at another time for your spiritual development you need to be engaged with social living as much as possible.

"Life then is unpredictable, changing every moment, externally but also inwardly, so I cannot structure life so fixedly including spiritual methods. I cannot say, I am going to structure today in a particular way. Some people think that a spiritual path should be rigid and structured."

Some structures are needed for people who have a lot of chaos. They may need some controlling factors. In that case some discipline may be helpful, but if you become spiritually mature you can be more flexible.

"Are you not returning to the topic of balance?" Keith asks. "You shared at an earlier time about the union of Shiva and Shakti. Are we not facing the possibility of uniting two principles? But the question also remains, what is behind these two primary principles? What or who is behind Shiva and Shakti?"

Behind natural polarities is natural Supreme Being that embraces all. It is not splintered reality. Sometimes I try to explain that only by meditation can I understand.

"This is important Yogi. But then the question arises, 'Is it enough to have this experience only now and then; isn't there a type of meditation that can produce more consistency? There are formal meditation practices, but is there another type of meditation that can be applied to any situation?"

Yes. I think it's an error when people have a narrow understanding of what meditation is. Many think it's a simple matter of sitting and trying to concentrate, but this can lead to inner tensions. Tantra accepts the different aspects of one's nature and is for spiritually mature seekers. This implies that practice can be wise and flexible as much as possible. We receive teachings all our lives but we must practice at the same time. Many think, 'First I should study how to practice and then do the exercises' but traditionally in India the student studied and practiced simultaneously.

"I wanted to ask you that. Can we bring these two things together: learning and practice?"

It must be like that. For instance, I first should prepare and after that a miracle can happen.

Jiva and Atman

Keith wants to explore further. "When in Hinduism the Jiva is referred to, is that the same ego as we Westerners understand it?"

It is not only ego, it is also when consciousness and life power including body awareness are dimmed by personal identification.

"Can we say that connecting to the Atman and Paramatman requires a sacrifice of the Jiva? Because it would seem that Jiva is where all the habits and tendencies are. If in heavy traffic it is the habit to experience road rage that is the Jiva. Jiva is then full of karmic patterns and tendencies. A reasonably thoughtful person might say, 'I understand that part of me and am aware of having many reactive tendencies and so on.' If I understand you correctly Yogi, there is a need to sacrifice some aspects of this conditioned Jiva in order to invite a greater peace and clearer experience. I need to de-identify with the Jiva. It is not who I really am. An over identification with the Jiva is the obstacle, is that correct?"

Yes, partly this is right, because the condition of Jiva is dependent, but also has good elements too. Therefore the ground of Jiva is actually

Atman, it is the same, as also Paramatman. They are connected layers of the same reality.

"So the aligned expression of the Jiva would be the natural personality?"

Atman is inside of the Jiva.

"Not Jiva inside of the Atman?"

You can say it like that too. It is whether the Jiva acts appropriately at any given moment. We all have the capacity to act appropriately. It is a matter of whether we do or not.

"If the Jiva's expression is inappropriate there would be a disturbance."

It is a matter of the point of view at any given moment. There can be the same situation but seen from different points of view, or different interpretations. For example, sometimes I choose not to share everything I am thinking when with a particular person. Maybe my words could have a hardening effect, or he may be incapable of digesting what is said, or simply cannot accept what I am saying. Some people may hear my words as hypocritical. Another person may listen and say to me, 'You are very wise.' It is exactly the same situation: the same words. Therefore I say regarding the Jiva, it is the expression of supreme and not different from the supreme. It is an aspect of the supreme.

"So Jiva doesn't see that it is the supreme?"

It is not aware. Awareness of the supreme is not present. You can say God created this body and mind and so on, everything is related to this incarnated physical 'me'.

Or you can say Jiva is God's excrement. It depends on how much wisdom people have.

Death and Life

Keith had something else on his mind. "Sigmund Freud said that there existed within a human being a death wish that he named 'Thanatos', the Greek God of Death. The implication is that there is an impulse to live but also a death wish. I imagine he observed this aspect in many people and perhaps also in himself. My understanding is that I can say yes or no to life. I can see God in the beauty of created life but then there is the other part that sees ugliness. The 'Thanatos' element may think that life is meaningless and purposeless. The Jiva can make bad choices if it believes life has no essential meaning. If I am going to die than nothing matters. Or maybe I don't like living. So many people commit suicide. Why so much homicide and suicide with seemingly no conscience or consideration of consequences? And look at how animals are mistreated in their countless numbers across our planet. It does appear as if there are two forces at play: a pro-life and an anti-life or pro-death force."

You cannot think about the beauty of life without simultaneously thinking about death. People are prejudiced because they are only afraid of death, but subconsciously many are also afraid of life. And yet life and death are inter-related. Some are so deeply afraid of life and prefer death. An exploration of life and death is a big mystery.

What is mystery? Mystery means something unknown for the mind. Everything unknown is most attractive, so behind this interest in death there is actually an attempt or desire to penetrate mystery. It is an enigma. What happens after my heart stops? My breathing stops when my body dies and it is no longer my body. What happens then? How do we exist in that moment?

It is a great enigma and we don't know, and therefore this topic becomes very attractive. Some people enjoy watching horror or scary movies and this can be understood. We should not criticize such people. We should understand this natural attraction that people have for these things.

The general, populist society, including psychiatrists or psychologists can say, 'These are crazy tendencies.' They might even say, 'You should take this medication so as to not think about such things. You should adopt a better way of thinking and conform to the social system. You should be better educated.' What is education? Many people cannot conform or adapt to society, this includes our youth.

People subconsciously are afraid of going crazy or being perceived as crazy. They fear that the social system will castigate them, therefore they try to follow what is expected of them, despite all the limitations.

If people follow all the requirements of the social system they end up thinking others who don't do so are crazy. So radical Muslim society think the Western life style is crazy. Or Westerners could think radical Hindus are crazy, for example, when they practice in cremation grounds. So if we extend our observation we can see that craziness is very common.

Life is so variable, but why can we not find the whole universe within ourselves?

"Is Gandhi's concept of 'ahimsa' harmlessness, related here? Are we not really crazy if we are not doing harm?"

I believe we are not crazy when we are aware of craziness especially including our own. If you are aware of much craziness, then who is it who is aware? Only that which is not craziness can be aware of craziness.

If you are not aware of craziness you become crazy. Then you have an actual identification with craziness. Those who say, 'I am not crazy' cannot observe themselves from another point of view.

Rabbit Holes and Fairytales

Rabbit holes are created by certain environments. There can be much variation within societies. The problem regardless of the situation is that the instrument thinks only 'it' is real. Yoga says you should always draw back a little. It's like withdrawing money and re-investing.

"During those years in India did you understand the need for flexibility, to have a flexible consciousness?"

Of course, it was most important. It was extremely natural. All atmospheres taught me that I should be flexible as much as possible, but not artificial. Again this is paradoxical, the need for structure but also flexibility.

"We are discussing about something real, and the possibility of experiencing and knowing it, and yet something simple. It isn't complicated. So what does it mean to be authentic? Ego may create much confusion but behind the confusion there is a simple reality. What that implies is that simplicity is our inborn nature. It is not something we create. We can see that in babies. They are simply being who they are until social conditioning adds layers."

It is paradoxical. Babies are innocent yet wise. Some people may have some skills. They may be very knowledgeable, smart, clever or intellectual: they maybe are academic and can answer questions, but sometimes they can become ignorant and stumble.

A yogi is like a baby. In Sanskrit, Sahaja can be understood as Saha, that means wise, and Ja means inherent. It implies being always aware of your inherent state, within everything that you are doing.

"So reality is not a fairytale. It is not getting lost down rabbit holes."

The fairytale is before you face reality. In India I thought this is like a fairytale, but when I examined it I thought, 'Russia is also a fairytale, another type of fairy-tale.' I smiled when I remembered something about Russia. In Russia they have their own illusions. In India they have theirs. And then they cannot understand each other. There is an Australian type of fairytale too.

But I cannot say all rabbit holes and illusions are bad. If consciousness acknowledges that everything is related everything happens perfectly.

Emptiness

Change is the nature of Shakti. Shakti is most important for Tantric Yoga. Actually static elements are important too, if they are properly understood. The immortal soul is static in a sense, and changing too. You can say eternity is static. What do we mean by static? You can move from here to there but emptiness is always the same. It is helpful to understand more clearly about what emptiness is. If you accept your ideas about emptiness, rather than actually experientially recognizing it, no psychologist or doctor can help you.

"Are we facing an essential problem in human psychology, that of our capacity for self-deception: self-deception being an action of creating an image of something, rather than experiencing reality?"

Yes.

"So can we say the greatest self-deception regards emptiness, but the experience is the essence of meditation?"

Yes, I think the experience of emptiness is the most profound within meditation. Emptiness is eternal and unchangeable. In Yoga you see static postures, so we should be stable in our posture of meditation.

We stop any type of disturbance, senses and movement. We try to stabilize the instrument of breathing, mind and body. We sacrifice everything to and therefore can be fully in emptiness. We can say it is a realization of emptiness even within activity. Emptiness should not become an intellectual mantra.

"Then it becomes the ground of our being."

Yes, it is omnipresent. Emptiness embraces fullness: that very changeable reality. If there is increasing realization of emptiness it means more freedom and increased capacity. There is more conscious choice.

Spiritual Practice

"What is spiritual practice?", asks Keith.

The word 'spiritual' is related to spirit and your soul, and what is most attractive for your soul. Most people enjoy intimacy but we ought not to be so fanatical about intimacy, because that which is pure can become rotten. Intimacy can become obsessive and corrupt attitudes; destroy fresh consciousness, all in the name of intimacy. Therefore it is good if we can talk about any topic including what it means to be crazy, and then such openness can be spiritual practice. With honest people you can make satsang.

"We are doing this anyway just by being naturally who we are. Everyone has this capacity but sometimes choose to engage in more useless activities."

If a person has no interest in life that's okay, but if I ask myself why should I settle for such limited experience and illusion, I can then choose to explore my human potential.

"To explore further suggests seeing the limitations of ideas, beliefs and habits. Would this not be an essential part of spiritual practice?"

That is freedom related with responsibility. With increased freedom there is more responsibility. There is no chance for ego. Ego in its problematic sense is when people stay unconscious. In consciousness there is no ego, one is very attentive. How can one be narcissistic if everything is inter-related?

There are many possibilities, much information, spiritual centers, organizations and books, and in that sense I know not everyone is coming to me and also I cannot pay attention to everyone. There is not enough time but we can all spend our time and energy for what is most sincere and important. Sincerity is important for spiritual development because then we can discuss any topic, including those that are often avoided. Practice needs to not be artificial. In this context, it is good that people have doubts. Not depressive doubts resulting from a need for definite black and white understanding, rather doubts that inspire one to study and research more and more.

Endings as Beginnings

"How would you like this book to end? What should be your final words?"

I laughed at this question and was silent for a few minutes.

The response must be unpredictable. For example, if I give you an answer it should be after I have read the book. So you can send it to me and I will see. I will meditate and see what comes and I will write it. And your task will be to polish the grammar, to arrange my crazy words.

My Guruji was often looking very weak and old but continued to write yet another book, but I was aware that it was not he that was actually writing these books, but rather by the Grace and power of Spirit or Supreme energy, that was writing through him. So surprisingly the books kept coming.

"I would like to suggest, what if we could live our lives like that? What if we could live our lives like a book or many books being written by Supreme Life?"

Something must happen in the best way, but we cannot create this by our ego, and yet we cannot avoid it either. This must happen. We can choose to avoid the dominance of ego as much as possible. Ego didn't create the galaxies and nature. There is a natural unfolding of spirit.

We can be very powerful according to how we surrender to Supreme power. If ego takes hold of this power it becomes immediately restricted. This is a part of spiritual practice.

People have different definitions and understandings about what is spiritual practice. Spiritual practice helps you be in your inherent wisdom. Inherent means in your nature. You are natural like a child, but wise. It is important because wisdom helps to avoid illusions. Illusion is ignorance. Ignorance is when one is not awake.

The background of your nature cannot be depressed. That which is most real cannot be depressed. Depression is like waves. Inherent nature is deeper than any waves. Sadness is a fog. Happiness is sunshine. But inherent nature is simply nature. Everything else, clouds, fog, sunshine and so on is inside of nature. Nature itself is not depression and you cannot say nature is good or bad. Nature is a deep static state. It is the deepest static that allows you to be more dynamic. This inherent static is not like the static of the instrument. It is not ego static. Ego static is a blocked version of your eternal soul.

In Yoga we view using different tools to enhance awareness, and bring you back to yourself. In that case practice becomes spiritual. If the tools are only for show or for their own sake, without understanding, then why accept them? Even if an experienced person who has experienced the true value of those tools, those practices, and understands that it is for his soul, his nature, and he can clearly give you examples, but if you are not experiencing it for yourself, then what is the value of it? If you are capable of receiving it he can give you an immediate experience. An intellectual person who gives many tools gives the menu, but not the food.

"But Yogi, even if someone has an experience in your presence they cannot be with you all the time. So how important is it to have a spiritual practice that is independent of being in the presence of a realized soul?

How important is it to take up a practice for oneself without relying on an external Guru?"

First we should understand that people do not exist in isolation. People's minds are created by society and this includes a lot of illusions. I am not thinking that I should give salvation to everyone: that would be a quite missionary approach. You should already have some inner experience. They should understand about what I teach, so there is a chance for them.

"Is that so that your influence can help to strengthen their practice?"

Yes. If I project my hope onto a person who is not ready I could become disappointed: and that person can be disappointed too. He might say, 'I didn't find anything valuable in all of this': or maybe valuable but nothing spiritual. If there are ingrained tendencies, maybe from past lives or anyway in his constitution, then we have a problem. He can only take what he is capable of taking and that's it. Maybe in the bigger picture he has another route. It is not my responsibility.

"So Yogi, every person is really responsible for themselves?"

Right! That is most important. Self-responsibility is vital. If people only talk about self-responsibility then they are fooling themselves. Then outcomes are unpredictable. If you put Buddha in front of such a one what use would that be? Two centuries ago some people hated Buddha. Some thought he was a heretic: same with Jesus and Gorakhnath. If people cannot accept then they cannot accept. That's it! That is life.

I heard a story about Buddha. One day Buddha came across a village. Locals decided to greet him. They brought him gifts, flowers and food. Buddha thanked them but said he didn't need anything, and therefore left everything and the festivities and continued on his journey. Along the way he came across another village. Its residents greeted Buddha with curses, mocked him and even threw stones at him. Buddha looked at them and said, "The inhabitants of a neighboring village greeted me with flowers and gifts. They arranged a festival, but I didn't take anything. I left behind all they gave. Now, I am going away from your village without taking anything too. What will remain with you after my leaving?" One villager asked, 'why did you say thank you?' He said, "Before you I visited another village where most complimented me. Their compliments were mundane and hypocritical. I said thank you to them. So I say the same to you because I don't need their compliments or your criticisms."

Awakening

"If I am an average confused seeker, what is your advice? There are many seekers looking here and there: this teacher, that seminar, that book, these methods, but they are still unstable and confused. There is something missing. They understand intellectually but ask how is this done? How is it possible? How can a shift happen, just like that? Say I am anxious or confused, and desire to shift into being calm and peaceful. I want to be back in 'that' experience that I've tasted before, but right now my car has broken down or my partner has walked out on me or someone close has suddenly died or I am in debt. Maybe I have chosen unwisely and have created difficulties for myself. I accept responsibility for that but am still asking 'is it possible to invite a meditative experience?' Can I shift from confusion and anxiety to a calm meditative state of being? Maybe I am not in a position to formally meditate. What do you do Yogi when confronted with unexpected and difficult circumstances? You wanted this biography to be very honest. How do you meet your biggest challenges?"

I believe we already possess wisdom. Many teachers do not address this need for immediate awakening. They do not address the means for awakening that you already possess. They do not give what you need to awaken. Real teachers create a sense of the topic: an atmosphere conducive to knowing how to listen and becoming self-aware. Being self-aware is what is most important. Of course we should be aware of everything surrounding us because everything is inter-related. Behind everything that appears accidental and random there is supreme consciousness, which arranges everything. This is very difficult to describe.

It is a matter of listening to oneself. Awareness happens at the same moment as such inner listening.

Imagine sitting in a car amidst heavy traffic. You should be aware of the status of your car, people, and the mobile phone that is calling you, the other traffic and general surroundings. You could say, 'I am only driving', but actually many things are happening that you could potentially be aware of. Sometimes in such a situation you could make a mistake, some element that becomes problematic. In this situation everything is unpredictable, and there are various possible consequences that could affect your future. Therefore one should be aware throughout of what is happening, moment by moment.

If we believe in Supreme Self that is omnipresent and is everywhere, then we can see with spiritual eyes. Supreme Self and self are together: Atman and Paramatman. So this is the challenge: how much attention should we pay and to which feelings, processes, nature and so on.

Then miracles can happen, especially during big challenging times.

It is a matter of listening to oneself. Awareness happens at the same moment as such inner listening.

Epilogue

It's almost two years since Keith and I began the biographical journey that led to this book. Much has changed during that time for both of us. The project began for me in Warburton in the state of Victoria, Australia and ended in Woy Woy, New South Wales. A condition of my visa was to reside for two years in New South Wales if I wanted to apply for Australian citizenship. I received citizenship in May 2017. I am no longer a homeless refugee and as significantly I can now travel without having to apply for visas.

It has been a great pleasure to collaborate with Keith and I'm very happy with the end product. As I wrote to him after receiving and reading the printed proof copy, 'The book is fantastic. If it would not be me and I read this book, maybe I would become a follower of myself.'

I appreciate the relevance of the questions asked and topics raised that have brought my story to life in ways that can feed the soul of the reader.

I offer this in good faith, and with blessings from the heart.

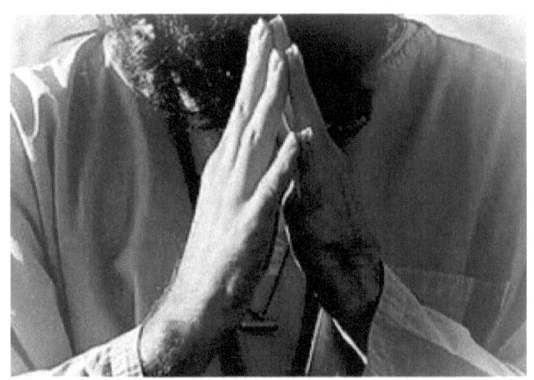

nathas.org